Confidence • Narrowcasting • Lav
bicle Monkey • Firing on All Cylinde
mark • Parameters • Thinking Outside
e Plan • Learning Curve • Nerve C
ased • Green ... ... • ETA •
n-Up • ... ... ction •
on D ... ... set-Purc
ent ... ... pin • IP
-Trus ... ... manager
• Squ ... ... gm Shif
Get wi... ... cture • U
ayering • Functional Flexibility • Pro
lysis • Bottom Line • WOMBAT • Ba
Face Time • Movers and Shakers
e Bar • Glass Ceiling • Downshifting
• Hands-On/Hands-O
MBWA • Window

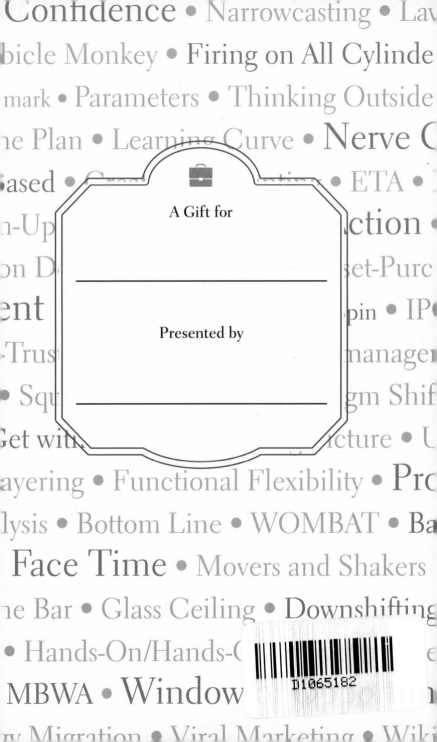

A Gift for

_____

Presented by

_____

D1065182

In the Loop
&
Up to Speed

In the Loop
&
Up to Speed

Clever and Useful
Business Terms Every
Go-Getter Needs

CAROLINE TAGGART

The Reader's Digest Association, Inc.
New York, NY / Montreal

A READER'S DIGEST BOOK

Copyright © 2011 Michael O'Mara Books Limited.

First published in Great Britain by Michael O'Mara Books Limited, 9 Lion Yard,
Tremadoc Road, London SW47NQ

Library of Congress Cataloging in Publication Data
Taggart, Caroline, 1954-
  In the loop and up to speed : clever and useful business terms every go-getter needs /
Caroline Taggart.
          p. cm.
  Includes bibliographical references and index.
  ISBN 978-1-60652-518-0 (alk. paper)
 1. Business–Terminology. I. Title.
  HF1002.5.T34 2012
  650.03–dc23
                                    2012010911

We are committed to both the quality of our products and the service we provide to our
customers. We value your comments, so please feel free to contact us.

            The Reader's Digest Association, Inc.
            Adult Trade Publishing
            44 S. Broadway
            White Plains, NY 10601

For more Reader's Digest products and information, visit our website:
            www.rd.com (in the United States)
            www.readersdigest.ca (in Canada)

Printed in the United States of America

1 3 5 7 9 10 8 6 4 2

Contents

Introduction

A friend approaching retirement was recently asked by a colleague if he was "grooming an exit strategy." Someone unfamiliar with modern idiom who overheard this conversation might well have wondered if my friend owned a horse that he could ride out of town. Maybe after a daring bank robbery.

A teacher of creative writing described her students as "bright, serious, and **ENGAGED**." "Engaged?" our imaginary extraterrestrial might ask. "To be married? All of them?"

The same alien, reading in the business columns of a newspaper that "Working out the best **PACKAGE** can be complicated, as you can buy your broadband and landline separately or together, or buy a **BUNDLE** that also includes a digital television package," might be forgiven for thinking that he needed a supply of brown paper and string before he could invest in a home-entertainment system.

Jargon is an insider's language, a form of shorthand by which one member of a group communicates with another. Part of what makes it so baffling to outsiders is the way that it takes existing words and phrases and twists them for its own ends. Confusing as these language mutations may be to those outside the know, it is a natural evolution of words and expressions that need to be coined in order to cope with new ideas. Revolutionary new ideas that signal **PARADIGM SHIFTS** and grow **OUTSIDE THE BOX** to give the world **AGILE DEVELOPMENT** and **MALWARE, CROWDSOURCING** and **MASS SAMPLING**— terms to cover concepts that didn't exist fifty years ago but now flourish in the fluorescent lighting of offices around the globe.

Business jargon is built not just from board meetings but from the vocabularies of management consultants and marketing gurus, which produced **CORE COMPETENCIES, HORIZONTAL INITIATIVES,** and **MISSIONARY SELLING**. We outside the cubicle walls understand the individual words, but put them together into phrases and you have . . . well, some might say claptrap.

For years this was all *insiders'* claptrap, but in the last decade or two a funny thing has happened. Jargon has seeped out of the specialist area and begun sprouting up in everyday language. Where once only a techie would talk about something being **IN THE LOOP** and only a politician would be expected to be **ON MESSAGE**, nowadays we all want to be cc'ed on it. And much of the time, we don't have the slightest idea what it really means.

Marketing jargon may have its origins in a carnival parade (the **BANDWAGON EFFECT**) or corporate takeover may be salvaged by a character from a nineteenth-century children's novel (**WHITE KNIGHT**). Suddenly everyone's talking like they are out on the baseball field (**TOUCHING BASE**) or have an internal combustion engine (**FIRING ON ALL CYLINDERS**) in their brains.

This language may have been made up for fun (**WOMBAT**, short for "waste of money, brains, and time") or adopted because we are all so busy nowadays that we need to save nanoseconds when we're making deals **B2B** that require some **FACE TIME**. Some of it is imaginative, some annoying (no cross-reference needed here—just don't get me started). Some will pass into general language with it's ancestry forgotten, while others will disappear without a trace once they have served their purpose.

The aim of this book is to shed some light on a cross-section of these expressions; to see where they came from and how they got to where they are today; and to translate the gobblydegook into plain English. It will sometimes be appreciative, sometimes irritable, but even at its grumpiest it will give credit to the versatility of the English language and to the people who keep **PUSHING THE ENVELOPE** of semantics.

1

Considering Your Position

GETTING A JOB, LEAVING A JOB, AND
THAT AWKWARD TIME IN BETWEEN

There's jargon attached to interviews and recruitment and
jargon attached to getting rid of people. There's jargon attached to actually doing the job, too, from the time you're
sitting at your desk generating a report—or whatever it is
people do at desks—to the time you're at a meeting pretend-
ing there's an upside to the plunging red line in your report.
This chapter considers some of the strange language we use
to cover all these situations.

Brain Dump

"To dump" in the sense of "to copy data to another, usually
external, location for security or back-up purposes" has been
around since the 1950s, and it is this meaning that has been
adopted into the "brain dump." It's a useful concept if you
are leaving a job: You want to download everything pertinent
that is in your brain into a format that your successor can

absorb. Since USB port implants for the cerebral cortex won't be out for another year or two, this usually takes the shape of a haphazard collection of the sort of stuff you might have produced if you were interpreting the word "dump" in quite another way. Such a word choice makes it easy to see that lurking in the subtext of this expression is the idea that you are glad to be getting out and frankly past caring.

Brownie Points

When I was in the Brownies, you didn't get points; you got badges for achievements in various fields such as cookery or starting campfires without endangering life and limb. No

11

matter. Brownie points is the expression that entered the language about fifty years ago. To gain them means that in some way you have successfully sucked up to the boss and will be viewed more favorably from now on. Brownie points have nothing to do with **KPI**s or any of the other "measurables" so beloved of management consultants (see **DASHBOARD**)—they are by definition nebulous and may be awarded or withdrawn at any time, often without your knowledge.

Considering Your Position

In business or politics, this is almost always followed by a resignation. Considering your position is something you have to do when the management has **MOVED THE GOALPOSTS**, **DOWNSIZED** your department, or otherwise made it clear that they are thinking of **LETTING YOU GO**. If you are in the public eye, it is possible that you have done something scandalous and no one is prepared to **DRAW A LINE UNDER IT**. Whatever the circumstances, you are likely to be spending more time with your family in future.

Cubicle Monkey

As early as 1682, a monkey could be "a person engaged in any of various trades and professions, especially one performing a subordinate or menial task or one that involves physical agility." The oldest usage in this sense is "powder monkey," meaning someone carrying gunpowder from the store to the guns themselves, particularly on a warship. Later there were grease monkeys, who mended cars and got covered in grease; bridge monkeys, who built bridges; and road monkeys, who repaired logging roads. In the United States in the nineteenth century, "monkey" was also thieves' slang for an associate or an unknown stranger. In Britain there was the organ grinder, whose less-skilled companion was—literally—a monkey.

Take any combination of these attributes and remove the positive qualities of those born in the Chinese Year of the Monkey: liveliness, ambition, opportunism, and entertainment value. Put them behind a low partition in an open-plan

They're not pretty, but they are cheap.

office and—hey, presto!—you have a cubicle monkey: an unappreciated functionary performing an endless stream of routine tasks. If you feel such a creature needs sustenance at any time, refer to the entry on **MUSHROOM MANAGEMENT** for advice on its diet.

Ducks in a Row

In bowling terminology, a duck or duckpin, first recorded in 1911, is "a small pin shorter than a tenpin but proportionately wider at mid-diameter." When you line such pins up—in a row—you are ready to roll, so to speak. If you do the same thing metaphorically, you have everything neat, tidy, and organized. Your arrangements are completed, your in-box is under control, your filing is done, and goodness your colleagues must hate you.

Elephant in the Room

Here's an expression that has evolved in an interesting way over the last fifty years. The *Oxford English Dictionary*'s earliest citation, from the *New York Times* in 1959, is "Financing schools has become a problem about equal to having an elephant in the living room. It's so big you just can't ignore it." However, in modern usage the whole point of an elephant in the room is that you do ignore it. It's too big, too uncomfortable, too controversial to do anything other than pussyfoot around it until someone gets sat on.

Entry Level

The earliest use of this dates back to the 1950s and refers to the basic level at which a job or academic course may be entered and the minimum qualifications or experience required. At entry level you might be given a job for which you had no obvious qualifications but were deemed to have potential, something like making copies, getting coffee, or other forms of menial gofor'ing.

From this, the use of "entry level" has expanded to describe a product or activity suitable for a beginner: an "entry-level computer" would be **USER-FRIENDLY** to the technologically challenged, while an "entry-level adventure vacation" might suit someone who had never walked on hot coals before but felt they were up for an exciting new challenge.

(Taking Your) Eye Off the Ball

This is a metaphor from the world of sports and was first recorded in the 1930s. It means, of course, to let your attention wander and to lose sight of your objectives. Maybe you were daydreaming about your co-ed kickball league and screwed up some decimal placements; or it could be that your thoughts were a little groggy because you woke up for a five a.m. tee time, and you ended up operating on the wrong knee. No matter what ball your eye wandered from, when you make this mistake, the results are to a greater or lesser extent catastrophic—and you certainly weren't being a team player.

Fast Track

The original "fast tracks" were those at racetracks that hadn't been rained on lately, so horses were able to run quickly over the hard ground. By 1970, the expression had moved into the business world. It was initially used as an adjective to describe an individual likely to be promoted rapidly or a training program such a person might take. Shortly afterward it became a verb: Drugs to combat highly publicized diseases (as opposed to **ORPHANED** ones) might be "fast-tracked" on to the market. Promising **ENTRY-LEVEL** office workers might be "fast-tracked" into executive positions, or, more often, relatives of the boss who are entry-level might be "fast-tracked" into executive positions.

You also see the word on signs at the passport-control and security areas of airports, where it simply means that those traveling business or first class—possibly people who live life in the fast lane—can jump the line.

Fire-Fighting

Fires are emergencies that need to be dealt with immediately, and they can take on many different forms. They can be a computer bug, a breach in security, or a crisis at the copier that should be printing the catalogue for an exhibition that opens tomorrow but is instead stubbornly jamming every paper it gets its maws on. Serious problems arise when every day brings a new fire: there is no time for planning, consolidation, back-up, or the implementation of strategy because everyone is running around dousing the copy machine and rescheduling exhibitions.

This modern meaning of fire-fighting—"dealing with events as they occur, without long-term planning"—seems to have arisen as recently as the 1990s, perhaps in response to the **DOWNSIZING** of many corporations. At that time, those still in employment were routinely working ludicrous hours so they could do both their own jobs and those of the people who had been **LET GO**. Fire-fighting was the only way to cope.

The experts tell us that too much fire-fighting shows a lack of organization and draws resources away from areas that were at one time functioning perfectly well but are then sucked inexorably into the chaos catch on fire themselves. What is needed is **DRP**.

Gagging Clause

Here's an unusual thing: an expression that is not a sugar-coated euphemism (see, for example, **GARDEN LEAVE**) but a gloves-off, no-messing-around piece of contractual terminology. Gagging or gag clauses may be found in a number of contexts, most notoriously in the now illegal medical practice of not presenting a patient with all the options for treatment because some of them are deemed too expensive. This "gag" was imposed on individual physicians by the Health Maintenance Organization that controlled their budgets.

The ex-spouses and ex-nannies of celebrities may also find themselves bound by gagging clauses, preventing them from selling their stories to the popular press. What a shame. Imagine if Brangelina's nanny could talk!

In employment law, if you have a gagging clause in your contract, you are forbidden from revealing confidential information to journalists, competitors, and the pretty blonde at the bar of the convention center who has taken a surprising interest in what exactly you do. Careless talk costs jobs, in other words.

Garden Leave

A euphemism, in use since the 1980s, for sending someone home on full pay—normally to run out the time they have

left before being let go—without actually doing any work. In other words, you want to get rid of him, you don't want his agitated influence in the office, but if you fire him, he'll sue. The implication is that he will have plenty of time to relax in his garden, which will keep him out the way and, specifically and often contractually, prevent him from selling his expertise to your competitors (see **GAGGING CLAUSE**). It's a bit like house arrest, but with fewer guards. And more chilled drinks in the backyard.

Apologies for the sexist use of pronouns here: women may be sent on garden leave, too, but generally only if they have conquered the barriers of the **GLASS CEILING** and the **MARZIPAN LAYER**.

Glass Ceiling

An invisible barrier to advancement, usually applied to women and minority groups who fail to get promotions beyond a certain level because of their gender, ethnicity, or other target for prejudice. Such people can see the next step in their career, and maybe some unsettling underbellies, but they just can't seem to become members of the boys' club, which usually comprises the entire population of the rooftop party above the glass ceiling.

Gay Bryant, author of *The Working Woman Report* (1985), may have been the first to use the expression when she wrote:

Partly because corporations are structured as pyramids, with many middle managers trying to move up into the few available spots, and partly because of continuing, though more subtle, discrimination, a lot of women are hitting a "glass ceiling" and finding they can rise no further.

In the quarter century since those words were written, increasing numbers of women have penetrated the glass ceiling only to find themselves bogged down in the **MARZIPAN LAYER**.

(Moving the) Goalposts

The origins are obvious: moving the goalposts on a sports field makes it more difficult to score a goal. The *Oxford English Dictionary*'s earliest quotation (1958) suggests that the expression was first meant positively, as a way of stimulating students to set higher goals. Nowadays, moving the goalposts—whether political, financial, or ethical—is almost invariably seen as unfair. Sometimes there's even a moving target inside the moving goalposts, making the odds of scoring about as good as that of a snowball surviving in hell.

Golden Handshake

All that glitters may not be gold, but there is certainly a lot of the glittery stuff being passed around when people change jobs. A golden handshake is a payout given to someone upon retirement (as a reward for long and faithful service) or upon leaving a job for some other reason (usually being canned but having such a watertight contract that canning without vast remuneration is not an option—see **GARDEN LEAVE**).

This concept was first recorded in 1960 (to be followed some fifteen years later by "golden handcuffs") to cover the benefits, perhaps in the form of bonuses, share options, or pension arrangements, that made it undesirable for a valued employee to leave. Then in the 1980s came the "golden parachute," a guarantee of financial protection for senior management in corporations threatened with takeover. Finally the "golden hello" was born, which is another (inevitably substantial) sum paid to an already high earner, such as a company executive or a football player, as an inducement to change jobs or teams. Why this is not called simply a bribe is a matter for debate.

The recipient of a "golden hello" is obviously a golden boy (or girl, though the **MARZIPAN LAYER** makes this less likely), but there is a warning attached to the term: It loses its luster all too quickly. The playwright Clifford Odets coined "golden boy" in his play by the same name. The lead character enjoys a brief flurry of success as a prizefighter, but on his way to the top, his desire to win overpowers all the qualities that made him a decent human being, and he is eventually killed after he speeds off in the flashy car he had bought with his winnings. If you've seen the film and remember a happier ending—well, that's Hollywood's golden age for you. And see **CASH COW** for a reminder of the dangers of killing the goose that lays the golden egg.

Heads-Up

A warning given benevolently by one colleague to another, so that the latter can be prepared for something that is about to happen, as in: "I'll give you the heads-up on the sales figures before the meeting, so you can decide to bring champagne or excuses."

"Heads up" was originally a military order, short for "lift your heads up." From here it developed into an adjective meaning "competent, in the know." As in, "She was a very heads-up teacher, always looking for new ways to keep the children awake." By the 1970s, still as an adjective, it came to mean "in the form of an advance warning." If you were a solid-gold employee in the disco decade, you might have gotten a heads-up memo that was circulated to a chosen few before some news was made public. The current usage of the term as a noun was first recorded in the early go-go '80s.

Hitting the Ground Running

Be afraid when you hear this phrase in a job interview. Be very afraid. The company, or at least the area you are being invited to join, is in chaos. It is understaffed and under-organized. There will be no training. There will be no handover period with the previous incumbent, because he or she has been LET GO as a result of causing the chaos in the first place. There will be no suggestion of being broken in gently, finding your feet, or feeling your way. You will be expected to know the job inside out from day one. Did I mention that you should be afraid?

Using this expression in the literal sense dates back more than a hundred years to the time when you were expected to hit the ground running as you leapt from a train, presumably because you were given a pink slip by the train guard.

Knee-Jerk Reaction

If you are sitting down with your feet off the floor and someone taps you just below the knee with a small hammer, the lower part of your leg jerks forward. Physiologically, this is a knee-jerk reaction—a reflex that you don't make consciously and can't prevent. Also called the patellar reflex, it's been known in medical circles since the early nineteenth century, and it means that the tendons that control the knee are functioning properly, which is a good thing.

In business and politics, however, where the expression has been used since the 1960s, a knee-jerk reaction is generally a bad thing: a reaction made automatically, without thought, and often in a panicky **MIND-SET** to deflect blame onto a nearby whipping boy or girl.

Let Go

Except on reality shows, almost no one is fired these days. At least not in so many words. Being let go is the business equivalent of being told by a boyfriend/girlfriend, "It's not you, it's me," or, "I just need a little more space." Wrap it up in fancy wrappings as much as you like, you are still being dumped. Similarly, "We're going to have to let you go," "We need to adapt our staffing levels to current market conditions," or anything that has the word **DOWNSIZING** in it all boil down to the same thing: You're out.

Level Playing Field

Playing on a level field is like knowing where the goalposts are (see **(MOVING THE) GOALPOSTS**): It makes the game a whole lot easier and fairer. As with **TOUCHING BASE**, there is no early-recorded example of the expression being used literally. This one sprang fully formed into the world of metaphors in the 1970s. So ingrained in the vocabulary

has it become that there is now a Level Playing Field Institute, based in San Francisco, whose vision is "a world where everyone has access to opportunities, including the historically disenfranchised"—in other words, "a world where a true level playing field exists." Among other things, LPFI offers a Summer Math and Science Honors academy (SMASH) and an Initiative for Diversity in Education and Leadership (IDEAL). So, highly commendable though its vision obviously is, the institute is not above contorting the names of its courses to produce improbably positive acronyms.

25

Marzipan Layer

A recent coinage, credited to Sylvia Hewlett of the Center for Work-Life Policy, to describe the sticky area just below boardroom level above which few women manage to rise. Although there are many accomplished women in not quite the top jobs, only 3 percent of the Fortune 500 corporations have female CEOs. Sylvia maintains that this is because women lack the "sponsorship" of powerful people (usually men) who will back them all the way. This is due largely to a woman's ipso facto denial of membership for the boys' club, which would get them onto the golf courses they'd need to tee off on in order to be privy to the meetings where the real decisions are made. (See also GLASS CEILING.)

Methodology

At the start of a thesis or other academic paper, it is traditional to detail what you were setting out to establish, how you collected and analyzed your data, how this enabled you to draw your conclusions, and why this was the best way of going about it. This is a methodology. So important is it in academic circles that there are innumerable websites offering students advice on how to write one clearly and accurately.

What a methodology *isn't* is a method. So to say "When preparing a presentation, my usual methodology is to make notes, expand on the key points, then throw in a few jokes" is to use jargon of the worst kind. In a world where saving fractions of a second seems so important to so many people (see all of Chapter 6) it is surely crazy to use a word of five syllables when a word of two would not only do perfectly well, but would be more accurate and less pretentious.

Mind-Set

A mind-set started out as much the same as "a set mind"—a fixed attitude or way of doing things. Used by psychologists from the early years of the twentieth century to describe someone who was stuck in their ways, it moved into common parlance by the 1960s. Since then it has since been taken up by life coaches, who—as is their wont—have put a positive **SPIN** on it. Nowadays the right mind-set can ensure that you are successful at work, happy at home, vice versa, or both. From being an inflexible barrier to development, it has become something that can itself be developed to make you into the dynamic, charismatic person you always knew you really were.

Package

You might think that a package would be the same as a bundle (see **BUNDLING**), and so in a sense it is: a "vacation package" offers several services in one—flight, hotel, car rental, excursions. In the business world, however, "package" has turned into an abbreviation for two very different things. As an inducement to join a company you might be offered an attractive "package"—not just salary but health benefits, generous paid holidays, and so forth. When times are tough and they need to **LET YOU GO**, your "package" means a redundancy package in which they pay you a little bit of money after they lay you off, presumably so you're less likely to raise an expensive legal ruckus. (See also **DELAYERING**.)

Pushing Someone's Buttons

This is not exclusively a business term, as you can push the buttons of your nearest and dearest as well as the guy who sits behind you and hates your talk radio station. The idea of pushing a button to make something like a doorbell work has been around since the late nineteenth century. The

suggestion that a person has buttons which, when pushed, would not merely annoy them but would really *really* touch a nerve seems to have evolved as early as the 1920s—perhaps around the time when doorbells had gotten nearly every person who owned out of the tub more than once. However, like **ETA** (particularly in Portugal), this is an expression that should be used with care in the workplace, because "pushing someone's buttons" can also mean to turn them on in the sexual sense—and charges of harassment have been brought for sillier reasons.

Raising the Bar

This has its origins in high-jumping and pole-vaulting: after each round of a competition, the bar is raised so that the remaining contestants have to jump or vault ever higher. Since the 1970s it has been widely used in a metaphorical sense to mean to aim for a higher standard. It's also possible to lower the bar. Such a feat can work to your advantage if the person who had your job before you had it did such an awful bar-lowering job that just showing up and not drooling earns you a bonus.

Self-Starter

In the employment world, a self-starter will **HIT THE GROUND RUNNING** and be able to **FIRE ON ALL CYLINDERS** without the need for **MICRO-MANAGEMENT**. In other words, a salesman will be capable of picking up the phone and approaching potential new clients; a journalist will have ideas for stories; a lawyer will have already billed future clients. However, the moment the person has entered employment the expression will be dropped, as it is almost never used outside the want ads.

Like firing on all cylinders, the image comes from the early days of the automobile, when a vehicle with a self-starter was more sophisticated than one that had to be cranked with a starter handle. The figurative use has been around since the 1960s, the decade when initiative and individuality were prized above all other qualities, except for maybe hair length and bell-bottom width.

Shooting the Puppy

In his book *Shoot the Puppy*, Tony Thorne, Language and Innovation Consultant at King's College London, traces this expression's origins to the 1980s American game-show producer Chuck Barris. Chuck apparently speculated about how desperate people were to appear on television and came up with a fantasy format that involved asking members of the studio audience to shoot a puppy out of the arms of a small child. What he wanted to know was how much (or little) money would it take to get people to do this appalling thing, just to gain those few seconds of fame. For some reason this format was never made into a long-running series, so we can only continue to wonder about the answer to Chuck's question.

Moving on from this inauspicious start, shooting the puppy means "taking the most extreme action imaginable" when, to quote Tony Thorne, things have gone "several steps beyond . . . 'biting the bullet.'" In a business context it can be a positive thing: making the really tough decision that just has to be made but is very much the last resort, to be taken only after **DOWNSIZING** and **GOLDEN HANDSHAKES** have failed.

Synergy

This has meant "working productively together" for several hundred years, but it went through a number of specialist

31

meanings before reemerging into the world of jargon. Muscles synergize to produce a required action in the body; a combination of drugs synergizes to become more effective than any one of them would be individually. But nowadays—and from as long ago as the 1950s—a group of colleagues or business partners can combine to produce synergy. What you or I might call "better results."

Time Poor, Cash Rich

This was the great cry of the over-worked, over-stressed 1980s when it seemed like lots of people had plenty of money but no time to spend or enjoy it. How times change. But, as one encyclopedia of management wryly points out, being time poor but cash rich is really a lifestyle choice, while those who are time poor *and* cash poor rarely have any say in the matter. (See also **WORK-LIFE BALANCE**.)

Touching Base

This translates as "calling up to say hello because we haven't been in touch for a while" or "attending the same meeting ostensibly in order to maintain close contact, but in actuality it is so brief it borders on pointless." The expression dates from the early twentieth century and, surprisingly, there is no previous recorded use in a literal sense from the world of baseball. But that is where it originates: A batter must touch a base as he runs around the diamond. If he is hoping to score a home run he passes each base very quickly and with only the most token "communication."

Up to Speed

This started its life in the nineteenth century as a literal expression used for a racehorse or a car running at full speed, or at least as fast as you could reasonably expect it to go. By the 1970s "to bring someone up to speed" was a substitute for "to brief them, fill them in on the latest developments" and so it has remained. It's not dissimilar to keeping someone **(IN THE) LOOP** in the hope that they will **GET WITH THE PROGRAM** and be **(ON) MESSAGE**.

Upping Your Game

Unlike **RAISING THE BAR**, this is not deliberately setting a new challenge for yourself. Instead, the new challenge has been set for you, and you have to play (or, in the literal sense, work) better and harder in order to achieve your goals. I say goals, but in fact the earliest uses of the expression refer to the goalpost-free game of tennis. Maybe this was said to people who had to hit the ball a bit higher so that it didn't smack into the net over and over again. Anyway, the expression had spread into the business world by the 1980s, and sales managers have been psyching up/terrifying their teams using this phrase ever since.

Watercooler Talk

This expression was first recorded in the 1990s and took off when it became a running gag in the comedy series *Seinfeld.* It was once the hallmark of a television program's success when "everyone" was talking about it in the office next day. Cynical producers were even alleged to insert controversial incidents specifically to make this happen.

Watercooler talk is not, however, restricted to conversations that begin with "Did you hear what happened on *Las Vegas Bride Hoarders* last night?" It could be office gossip, like the unbelievable promotion of Kathy from accounting who is clearly sleeping with someone because how else could she possibly get promoted.

By definition watercooler talk is any conversation that is unofficial, filled with juicy gossip about other people (real or otherwise), and gives coworkers common ground on which they bond.

Workshop

Originally a place where physical work was done, such as carpentry or schumackering, in the 1930s this word came to mean a meeting in which the participants took an active role. Early workshops tended to be in the arts, often promising "a friendly, supportive atmosphere," but today workshops are an integral part of management training. You can attend workshops in team building, communications, motivation, planning, and goodness knows what else. "Participation and

involvement increase the sense of **OWNERSHIP** and **EMPOWER-MENT**," claims one website, emphasizing the most important aspect of any workshop: You aren't allowed just to sit there and doze, or even just to sit there and take notes. That won't help your team-building skills one bit.

2

Blue-Sky Thinking

ACCENTUATING THE POSITIVE

In business it sometimes seems as if the worst thing you can today is to repeat the same thing you did yesterday. This chapter aims to celebrate and inspire those who think **IF IT AIN'T BROKE, DON'T FIX IT** is the enemy and who can't get through a work day without a good **CAFFEINE-FUELED BRAIN-STORMING** session.

Blue-Sky Thinking

This is one of many expressions in modern business designed to encourage people to **PUSH THE ENVELOPE, THINK OUTSIDE THE BOX**, and make the most of any **WINDOW OF OPPORTU-NITY.** However, in the early days—the 1960s and '70s—blue-sky thinking was something to avoid. It meant an idea was a pie in the sky that was unrealistic and fraught with difficul-ties, such as "the technology hasn't been invented yet" or "we don't have the money." That sense of caution was abandoned in the late twentieth century, and blue-sky thinking has now come to mean "The sky's the limit; let's go for it."

Brainstorming

This term is often considered non-PC these days, presumably because the original meaning of a "brainstorm" was a sudden disturbance of the mind, a "mental explosion" that might take the form of severe headaches or temper tantrums. Around the 1950s it was adopted into the non-medical vernacular to mean "thrashing out ideas through intensive, impromptu discussion," but in 2004 some overzealous new recruit to the Thought Police decided that it was offensive to those suffering from epilepsy.

The National Society for Epilepsy promptly and commend-ably carried out a survey that reported "93 percent of people with epilepsy did not find the term derogatory or offensive in any way and many felt that this sort of political correctness singled out people with epilepsy as being easily offended." So that's one win against the Thought Police.

Caffeine-Fueled

Caffeine is "an alkaloid that occurs naturally in tea, coffee, cocoa, and cola nuts, acting as a mild stimulant to the ner-vous system." In other words, it's the ingredient in coffee in particular that gives you a bit of a kick and can help keep you awake long enough to finish the task in hand. Caffeine-fueled is most often used in a somewhat bittersweet context. A caffeine-fueled meeting is one where everyone has taken suitable quantities of legal stimulants and is buzzing with bright ideas, enabling them to **PUSH THE ENVELOPE, THINK**

OUTSIDE THE BOX, yadda yadda yadda. . . . But underneath the chemical-energy high lies exhausted, groggy people who really need another couple hours of sleep rather than another couple cups of coffee.

Covering All (the) Bases

This is a term from baseball, in which a fielding player stands close to a base, ready to catch the ball if it is thrown to him, so that he is more likely to get the opposing runner out, thus "protecting against any eventuality." If all the bases are covered, the batting side is in a difficult position. In the business world the expression popped up in the 1990s, meaning that if you are covering all the bases, you are keeping your head in the game and making sure every possible anything has been forecasted and a plan has been formulated to deal with it. (See also **TOUCHING BASE**.)

Cutting Edge

Obviously knives have a cutting edge, but the figurative use of this expression—"a dynamic factor that gives an advantage"—has been around since the middle of the nineteenth century. Cutting-edge technology, which came along a hundred years later, metaphorically cuts through barriers and produces innovative ideas that put it at the forefront of its field. Nowadays it is not only technology that is cutting-edge;

the expression can be applied to, among other things, movies, or theater, art, and with the popularity of today's top chefs, even cooking. Regardless of the medium, someone is bound to lose a finger.

The foremost edge of a propeller blade, which does much of the work of shifting an aircraft forward, is called a *leading* edge; if you prefer to take your metaphors from aviation (as you may, if you are in favor of **PUSHING THE ENVELOPE**), you can substitute this for "cutting edge" without changing your meaning.

Downshifting

Not to be confused with **DOWNSIZING**, this is a voluntary action on the part of an individual who wants to achieve a better **WORK-LIFE BALANCE** by accepting lower pay in order to work

fewer hours and/or be in a less stressful job. It is satirized as meaning moving to Vermont to keep chickens, but it doesn't have to be that drastic: It could just mean moving to a smaller house in the same neighborhood.

In the nineteenth century, "downshift" could refer to any downward movement. By the mid-twentieth it was applied to downward trends in the stock market, consumerism, or other money-focused areas, as well as to slowing down the roll in a manual transmission car. The specific modern meaning evolved at the same time as the concept, around the 1980s when **TIME POOR, CASH RICH** was in its heyday.

Firing on All Cylinders

An internal combustion engine that is in optimum working order is said to fire on all (possibly four, possibly six) cylinders. The figurative use of the expression to describe someone doing an incredibly excellent job was first recorded in the early years of the twentieth century and was well established by 1932, when P. G. Wodehouse wrote, in his novel, *Hot Water*, "His smiling face, taken in conjunction with the bottle of wine which he carried, conveyed to Gordon Carlisle the definite picture of a libertine operating on all six cylinders."

In the business context, this is not the only cliché to be inspired by the internal combustion engine. Someone who is firing on all cylinders may well cause **SPARKS TO FLY** or be described as a **DYNAMO**. If he is just too full of **BRIGHT IDEAS**, he may cause his colleagues to blow a gasket.

Get with the Program

Surprisingly, this phrase has absolutely nothing to do with computing. It originally meant "to do what you are supposed to do." In a 1974 episode of the TV series *Columbo*, military trainees are woken at an ungodly hour with the cry, "Up and at 'em; let's get with the program"—it was time for them to get on with their duties, literally working through the program of the day's schedule. From this practical application the expression has been adopted into the workplace to mean "to make a positive contribution, to be on top of things," with the implication that you believe in and are prepared to go out and promote the company's ethos. Most recently it is said to employees to get them back on the right track or motivate them when they seem to be slacking. One's boss might say, "Johnson, I needed that report an hour ago. Get with the program, or you're going to get **DOWNSIZED!**"

Leading Edge

See **CUTTING EDGE**.

Learning Curve

Why a curve? Well, think back to high-school math and visualize the sort of graph where you plotted one value along the x-axis, another along the y-axis, and joined all the dots into a curve. (Didn't do that in school? Then you're facing a steep learning curve for understanding this entry.) Anyway, from the 1920s on, a graph like this was used by teachers and psychologists to illustrate someone's progress. The x-axis (along the bottom of the graph) conventionally indicated the time elapsed since the subject started school or entered employment, the y-axis (up the left-hand side) showed their level of competence. The steeper the curve, the faster they were learning.

Sometime in the last twenty years or so this technical term was adopted into informal language, so that "It was a steep learning curve for me" means "I had to learn a lot quickly, and it was hard." Or, as people who use this sort of jargon would say, "challenging."

Nerve Center

A term from biology meaning a group of nerve cells involved with a specific function from which individual nerves branch out. The figurative use is to denote the central point from which information or control flows dates from about the 1980s. Many groups often consider themselves to be nerve centers— IT, creative teams, management types—but it's much more debatable as to where the brains of the operation lay.

On Message

Simply put, being on message is being "in accordance with the ideas and policies of the political party, company, etc., to which you belong." The meaning can be applied to both an individual promoting the party line and the ability of the party itself to get its message across, often through the prudent use of **SPIN** doctors, media consultants, and the like. Employees who are not "on message" may be encouraged to **GET WITH THE PROGRAM**—or face the ignominy of being **LET GO** or sent on **GARDEN LEAVE**. The expression first emerged in US politics in the early 1990s and found its way elsewhere shortly after.

Pushing the Envelope

In aeronautical terms the "flight envelope" is the best possible performance you can get out of an airplane given its design—a combination of fastest speed, highest altitude, farthest range, etc. Engineers or test pilots who pushed the envelope were trying to extend these limits, to produce a plane that would fly faster, higher, farther. The author Tom Wolfe is credited with having popularized the expression in his book *The Right Stuff* (1979), but he didn't invent it—he quotes it as something that pilots said. Within a decade of Wolfe's using it, pushing the envelope had expanded beyond the field of aeronautics and was being applied to any pioneering endeavor that made the undoable doable or the unacceptable acceptable. See also **BLUE-SKY THINKING** and **THINKING OUTSIDE THE BOX**, and contemplate a bad joke heard somewhere: "No matter how much you push the envelope, it'll still be stationery."

Quantum Leap

To a physicist, a quantum leap is "the sudden transition of an electron, atom, etc., from one energy state to another"—a concept far too complex to go into here. To everyone else it is a spectacular advance, often skipping a stage that had previously been thought of as vital. So in physics it is a significant but tiny thing carried out at a subatomic level. Everywhere else it is huge.

The German physicist Max Planck first identified quantum physics in the early years of the twentieth century and won the 1918 Nobel Prize as a result. By 1930 physicists had given it the ability to leap, and by the 1950s the idea was jumping into the worlds of politics and business. (See also **PARADIGM SHIFT**.)

State of the Art

The first process recorded as being "state of the art" was photographic printing way back in the 1880s. Since then it has been in constant use for anything that scientific or technological skill can produce. In modern parlance this tends to be electronics (a "state of the art" mega-def television or 43G smartphone). Scientific and medical equipment ("state of the art" particle imploders) often get this red-carpet term. Whatever it is, you can be quite confident that it will look impressive, cost a fortune, and an even better one will be out this time next week.

Thinking Outside the Box

Did anyone ever think inside a box? It must have been an uncomfortable thing to do. Anyway, this expression emerged in about the 1970s, when sending executives on training courses became fashionable (management courses had been in existence since the 1930s, but kept a low-ish profile for their first few decades). These lucky execs would take a test of lateral thinking—another wildly popular business idea around this time—which consisted of a piece of paper on which there was a square containing nine dots. He or she was asked to join the dots using four straight lines without lifting pen from paper. Human nature, being the unimaginative thing that it is, usually assumes that the lines must be drawn inside the square. But no. The inventive, lateral-thinking, management-potential participant recognized that it was impossible to achieve the desired result unless you think (and draw lines) "outside the box." Aha!

Thinking the Unthinkable

This sounds as if it ought to be deplorable, like **SHOOTING THE PUPPY**, but in fact thinking the unthinkable is a positive, imaginative thing to do. Which is odd, really, because in the early 1960s "the unthinkable" meant nuclear war. Military strategist Herman Kahn popularized the expression with his book *Thinking About the Unthinkable* (1962) and was at the forefront of the policy of Mutually Assured Destruction—the idea that the only way to prevent a nuclear attack was for

45

the US to make it clear to the Russians that they too would be blasted to smithereens. Herman, by the way, was a student of game theory (see **ZERO-SUM GAME**), but it doesn't sound as if he would have been much fun to play with.

The expression got a new lease on life in British politics after Tony Blair became Prime Minister in 1997 and allegedly asked his Minister for Welfare Reform, Frank Field, to "think the unthinkable" with reference to the benefits system. Although subsequent events have cast doubt on what Mr. Blair intended, it seems safe to assume that he didn't mean "drop an atom bomb on it." By 2001 the expression was familiar enough to lend itself to the title of a radio sitcom in which a team of clueless management consultants,

Unthinkable Solutions, advised clients to implement weird and inevitably disastrous policies and lampooned pompous management speak while they were at it. If you hear a rustling in the distance, it is Herman Kahn turning over in his grave.

Work-Life Balance

In the mid-nineties pretty much anyone with a job was thought to be suffering from some form of work-related stress. Everyone—not just high-powered executives and working mothers—seemed to be reading their e-mails in the shower first thing in the morning in a desperate effort to keep on top of the chaos and then sending e-mails at eleven o'clock at night to show their bosses that they had true commitment and were still on the case when they should have been in bed.

So that just had to go. In its place came work-life balance. The expression was first recorded in 1977 but became part of daily language and angst-ridden newspaper articles only after the **INFORMATION OVERLOAD** brought about by e-mail. It means people taking a measure of control over when and how much they work, though the website worklifebalance.com wisely points out that there is no "perfect, one-size-fits-all" balance that everyone should strive for. It's up to you to decide where your priorities lie and how they might change at different phases in your life. In other words, are you happy to earn less in order to be able to relax more, or would you rather work yourself into an early grave in order to rake in an obscene salary? (See also **EMPOWERMENT** and **TIME POOR, CASH RICH**.)

3

An Executive Decision

It's the job of a company's higher-ups to see the **BIG PICTURE**
and have a long-term strategy for the business. They may not
always explain that to the rest of us, and they sometimes have
to make hard decisions along the way that seem awful. We
just have to have faith in them—or quietly berate them to
coworkers over **WATERCOOLER TALKS**.

Benchmark

Perhaps the only term in business jargon that comes from
surveying, benchmark originally meant "a mark on a post
or other permanent feature, at a point whose exact elevation
and position are known." Given that fixed point, you can—if
your math is up to it—calculate the elevation and position of
other points. And what about the bench? Well, a benchmark
was of a clearly defined shape, a broad arrow with a horizontal bar through it, and surveyors inserted an angle iron into
the bar, forming, according to the *Oxford English Dictionary*,

"a temporary bracket or *bench* for the support of the leveling-staff, which can thus be placed on exactly the same base on any subsequent occasion."

From this, the term broadened to mean a known point against which other things can be measured in any field. People have been using it this way since as far back as the nineteenth century, though most of us would not recognize a surveyor's benchmark if we sat on it.

Big Picture

In the early days of the cinema, the "big picture" was the main feature, the one starring people you had heard of, as opposed to the low-budget B movie that might be part of the same afternoon's entertainment. Since 1935 it has also been a "broad overview of a situation, a way of identifying overall aims and strategy." The boss—the one with the vision to see where the company will be in ten years' time—is a "big picture" person. She or he doesn't need or want to be bothered with details, and subordinates often are left wondering what she or he is doing all day in that big office.

It is up to the level of management below the big-picture thinkers to find ways of implementing the big-picture policies and carrying out the business on a day-to-day basis. However, if these people take their attention to detail too far, it will come under the heading of **MICROMANAGEMENT** and irritate their **DIRECT REPORTS**.

Broad Brushstrokes

There is no recorded use of this expression in the art world, but obviously if you paint with broad brushstrokes, you are not going to produce much detail and you'd be terrible at pointillism. (All those little dots? Not for me, thanks.)

Similarly, an executive who deals in broad brushstrokes does not exercise **MICROMANAGEMENT**. Around since the 1960s, this image can be approving or disapproving. After all, one person's visionary interest in the **BIG PICTURE** is another's careless lack of attention to detail. It all depends on where you are **COMING FROM**.

Corporate DNA

For a living being, DNA is a combination of the myriad elements that makes us the individuals we are. For a corporation it is much the same thing: core values, ethos, the invisible but fundamental aspects that make it unique.

The *Oxford English Dictionary* records a use of deoxyribonucleic acid from a scientific journal of 1944, although 1953 is the most famous date in the history of DNA: That is when Watson and Crick discovered the double-helix structure. It was fifty years later that the business world embraced the idea, and now they are truly taking it to heart, insisting that corporations are people too.

Dashboard

This used to just be the panel behind the steering wheel that showed you how fast you were driving and when you needed more gas (even before that, it was a mudguard on a horse-drawn vehicle). Then it became that handy application on an Apple computer that included a clock, a calendar, a calculator, the weather forecast, and more. Now it has been co-opted by management consultants, leading to claims such as "the top management dashboard is an effective means to monitor strategy execution and predefined objectives achievement. The dashboard structure definition, the selection of adequate **KPI**s, and their visualization are the key elements of this step." Knowing that **KPI**s are Key Performance Indicators will help you translate some of this into English, but only some of it. In a nutshell, it's about measuring performance in the workplace—something that performance-measurement consultants think is important and most other people regard as substantial five-figure sums down the drain.

Downsizing

At the time of the 1970s oil crisis, Americans, for the first time, were encouraged to drive smaller and more economical vehicles, and car manufacturers began to produce "downsized" models. Early uses of the term were very specific, talking about "shedding 6.5 inches of wheelbase" and increasing the amount of aluminum used in order to make the vehicles lighter. By the 1980s, however, the word had branched out from the automobile industry to include anything that might be made smaller, including a business. It wasn't long before that meaning was transferred from the business itself to the person who might be "downsized" or **LET GO** when the company tightened its metaphorical belt. The *Oxford English Dictionary*, in a draft addition dated March 2006, describes this usage as "frequently euphemistic or humorous." Events in the global financial sector since that date have likely led many people to think that it isn't very funny at all.

Executive Decision

This has its origins in nineteenth-century politics, where it meant "a decision made by the Executive" (that is, the

President's office) or by someone with executive power in their particular realm. For the last half-century or so it hasn't meant much more than "decision" and doesn't need to be made by an executive. But it does carry a certain amount of subtext: "I am going to make an executive decision" suggests that the subject has been discussed long enough and there is never going to be complete agreement. It is therefore time for somebody (it doesn't much matter who) to decide on a course of action that enables everyone to move forward. Ideology has failed, so pragmatism must take over. In fact, in most contexts you could substitute the word "arbitrary" for "executive" and not change the meaning appreciably.

Game Plan

Football players have had game plans since the 1940s, and the expression quickly spread out into the wider world. It means little more than a regular plan, but it has a reassuring ring that presumes the plan maker(s) actually took the time to think about the **BIG PICTURE** and come up with a strategy for all the team players. A game plan can be made for almost anything: you can have one for the company over the next five years or just to get through this afternoon's meeting.

Guidelines

A guideline was once drawn on a piece of wood to show the sawyer where to saw, or it was used on a template to show a designer or typographer how the words should line up on a page. It could also be a rope hung from a hot-air balloon or small aircraft to help with steering. Figurative guidelines, such as moral ones to keep us on the straight and narrow, have been around since the mid-twentieth century, and today you can find them for just about anything. Some companies have them for every aspect of employee life, from dress code to lunch hours to memo headings to e-mail signatures. But corporations have nothing on Uncle Sam, who has guidelines for ingrown toenails, the Internet, and everything in between.

Hands-On/Hands-Off

In the late 1960s—when avant-garde companies had a computer room with one vast computer in it and less avant-garde ones were still doing sums—not everyone could have direct experience of using the technology. Those who were able to sit down at a keyboard gained hands-on experience; the rest were lucky if they were given a copy of the manual to read.

Use of the term has broadened greatly since then, and you can have hands-on experience for almost anything, regardless of whether or not it involves using hands. By the 1980s companies were advertising "hands-on marketing **WORK-SHOPS**," suggesting that participants would do something other than sit and listen to a lecture. From here "hands-on" became a compliment for a manager who was prepared—normally metaphorically—to get his or her hands dirty by becoming involved in the practical aspects of a job, rather than sitting behind a desk and worrying about the **BIG PICTURE**.

The hands-on approach can, of course, be taken too far: see **MICRO-MANAGEMENT**.

Surprisingly enough, "hands-off" came into existence via a different route and lived a whole idiomatic life of its own before joining up with hands-on. In the early years of the twentieth century a hands-off policy was any policy of non-intervention, whether prompted by laziness or the result of a considered course of action. The arrival of aviation brought the concept of "hands-off" controls into the dictionaries in the 1930s. But "hands-off" management seems to have been created in about the 1990s as the opposite of "hands-on," with no specific reference to automatic pilots or policies.

(Playing) Hardball

In the nineteenth and occasionally the twentieth centuries, hardball was another name for baseball, for the not-rocket-science reason that it was played with a harder ball than softball. Aficionados of softball tend to be children, women, or non-serious athletes, while "real men" play baseball because, in the literal sense, they believe it's more masculine to play with the harder ball. In the figurative sense, they believe they can man-up by "using tough, uncompromising tactics in order to achieve your [their] ends." Whether or not playing hardball has ever gotten anyone anything other than high blood pressure and possibly an ulcer is up for debate. The metaphor has been around, mostly in North America, where the game and its vocabulary are endemic, since the 1970s.

Horses for Courses

If you are a fan of horse racing you will often hear television pundits remark that one horse will do well with a dry track (see **FAST-TRACK**), whereas the owners of another are hoping that it will rain overnight so that the ground is heavier. By extension, one horse may always seem to do well on a particular course which, for whatever reason, is suited to its style. In the business world, the same can apply to either a policy or a person—the former adapted to fit the circumstances, the latter chosen because he or she is suited to them. Racing correspondents were using this expression in the 1890s; the figurative sense came not long afterward and was used so frequently that it verged on cliché by the 1960s, proving it was the right horse for business discourse.

Keeping Your Options Open

This expression has been around for half a century, but where did it come from? No one seems to know for sure, but the most plausible explanation comes from the subsidiary meaning of option as "a right to conclude a financial transaction within a specified period." A stockbroker may take an option on certain shares, or a film producer may option a book that he may or may not later make into a film. The key here is that the decision to act must be made before a certain date, so if you keep an option open, you extend the deadline.

In the less formal sense, it may, of course, simply mean that you don't know the answer yet—perhaps you're waiting for a better option to come along—so you are trying to put people off until you know more.

Lose-Lose Situation

See **NO-WIN SITUATION**.

Mission Statement

This expression was originally a military one, referring to the objective of a particular mission or task. It had moved into

the business world by the 1980s, becoming a rather gran-
diose alternative to "what this company does." The Center
for Business Planning goes further in the grandiosity stakes.
It says that a mission statement should be a "clear and succinct representation of the enterprise's purpose for existence.
It should incorporate socially meaningful and measurable cri-
teria, addressing concepts such as the moral/ethical position
of the enterprise, public image, the target market, products/
services, the geographic domain, and expectations of growth
and profitability."

It's difficult to imagine how you can cover all that ground
and still remain succinct, but perhaps that is part of the
challenge.

Monitoring the Situation

In the early twentieth century, radio (and later television)
transmissions were monitored for quality without interrupt-
ing the service. During the World War II, the word acquired
an undertone of espionage, or at least of security. You might
monitor (read as eavesdrop on) a conversation, or maybe you
would monitor a convoy of ships to see where they were going
and what they were up to. The more general use of this saying
gradually evolved in the postwar years, so that now "monitor-
ing the situation" means "keeping an eye on it, to make sure
it runs along smoothly." It is, in a business sense, a perfectly
reasonable thing to do, not to be confused with "keeping the
situation under review," which has a pussyfooting ring to it
and is more closely related to **KEEPING YOUR OPTIONS OPEN**.

Movers and Shakers

These are the dynamic, active people who get things done. Unusually, we know exactly when this expression was first used: in a poem called *Ode* by Arthur William Edgar O'Shaughnessy, published in 1873. According to Arthur, the "music-makers" and the "dreamers of dreams," "world-losers and world-forsakers" are "the movers and shakers of the world forever, it seems." "One man with a dream" can achieve anything he sets his heart on, while the people who have no vision sit around and wait for someone else to tell them what to do.

No-Win Situation

A no-win situation is one in which—self-evidently—there is no possibility of anyone winning. It was first used in political circles in the 1960s, at about the same time as game theory (see **ZERO-SUM GAME**) was producing the happier win-win and less happy lose-lose situations. All three soon spread into the wider world.

Pan Out

As in "We'll see how it pans out," meaning "We'll see what happens." It sounds like a laissez-faire approach to business, but this attitude may be taken in the hope of striking gold. The expression comes from the days when prospectors washed quantities of soil in a pan in the hope of finding nuggets of shiny fortune. The first use—in the literal sense—dates from the California Gold Rush of the 1840s. In 1870 an early figurative use is attributed to Mark Twain, who wrote to his publisher, "January and November [sic] didn't pan out as well as December—for you remember you had sold 12,000 copies in December . . . But $4,000 is pretty gorgeous. One don't pick that up often, with a book." Considering that, according to one Consumer Price Index calculation, $4,000 in 1870 would equal $152,000 now, one sure don't. The book in question was *Innocents Abroad,* which became Mark's bestselling book in his lifetime and is still one of the bestselling travel books ever, so you never know how these things are going to pan out.

Paradigm Shift

A paradigm is an exemplar, stereotypical case. American author Robert Shea once wrote, "Military organization, like religious organization, can be seen as a paradigm of organization in general," which is a rare example of this much-abused word being used accurately. In science it also means the philosophical framework within which the theories, experiments, and so on take place. A paradigm shift is therefore a change in the concept or **METHODOLOGY** of such a school of thought. In the 1970s the term began to move away from the philosophy of science, into the world of technology and beyond. Over the years, inevitably, it has become corrupted. In a context such as "the industry is at a crisis point and a paradigm shift is required," paradigm has become simply a fancier sounding alternative to "fundamental."

Parameters

A parameter's origins are mathematical: in geometry, it once meant a chord in a circle, specifically (according to the *Oxford English Dictionary*) "the latus rectum, the chord bisected by and perpendicular to the transverse axis." You can see why that might not have caught on. By the nineteenth century it had developed a number of technical meanings in fields as wide-ranging as astronomy and crystallography, but in most cases it meant (roughly) a measurement that helped you to take other measurements. It had also, by the 1960s, been taken up by the music world. According to the

musicologist Joan Peyser, Robert Beyer, a pioneer of the use
of electronics in music production, borrowed the term from
mathematics "apparently to give weight and dignity to what
otherwise would be called an element or dimension." From
there "parameter" has been adopted into common vernacular to give weight and dignity to what might otherwise be
called **GUIDELINES**: rules or restrictions imposed by schedule
and budget.

(In) Real Terms

This started life in the mid-twentieth century as an economic concept, meaning what money could actually buy
rather than any nominal or theoretical value. For the non-
economists among us, the *Oxford English Dictionary* gives this
example from 1976: ". . . Canadian business receives about
as much in federal subsidies as it pays in federal income
tax—and thus contributes practically nothing, in real terms,
to running the government." Since that time the expression
has penetrated so far into day-to-day business speak as to be
practically meaningless: "What are we doing, in real terms?"
means very little more than "What are we doing?" though it
does perhaps imply an element of "Cut the crap, won't you?"

Spin-Offs

In the 1950s, spin-offs were shares in a new company distrib-
uted to the stockholders of a parent company; from there the

expression came to refer to the new subsidiary company itself. Then it went on to be applied to people striking out on their own, and also (yet entirely unrelatedly) benefits or discoveries emerging from a technological development. Teflon, for example, can be regarded as a spin-off from research into CFC refrigerants. Call it a by-product, a side effect, or an accident if you prefer.

The specific usage to describe a new TV series centering on some of the same characters from an old one, as *Joey* was a spin-off from *Friends* or *Torchwood* from *Doctor Who*, evolved from this sense and emerged in the 1960s.

Squaring the Circle

Geometry specialists through the centuries have tried to create a square that has the same area as a given circle. Why? No one knows. Perhaps they liked the process's formal name, which is quadrature. Anyway, in the nineteenth century somebody managed to prove that it was impossible. It has to do with the transcendental nature of pi, *obviously*. So, while the mathematicians may have given up trying, the expression has been adopted into real life to mean "any impossible task."

Swarm Intelligence

Gerardo Beni and Jing Wang introduced the metaphor of swarm intelligence in the 1980s to describe part of their robotics systems. Drawn from bees, it has to do with lots of parts working together—as in a hive or an ant colony—to a common end, without any one individual knowing what the **BIG PICTURE** is. And also robots. Soon after its introduction, it spread out through the medium of science fiction and the *Matrix* films into the wider world. You can also have swarm factors and swarm logic, and though no one really understands them, they are generally a bad thing. We'd have no honey in the world without them.

Talk the Talk, Walk the Walk

Sometimes abbreviated to "walk the talk," this is not a far stroll from "put your money where your mouth is," but in a good way. To talk the talk is to convey company policy articulately and convincingly if not necessarily sincerely. To walk the talk is to put it into action, particularly when it comes to "ethical, values-driven leadership." As Eric Harvey, founder of walkthetalk.com, puts it, "People hear what we say, but . . . seeing is believing."

Win-Win Situation

See **NO-WIN SITUATION**.

Zero-Sum Game

This is a situation in which the gains and losses add up to zero: the winner can gain no more and no less than the loser loses. So this is neither **WIN-WIN** nor **NO-WIN**, but something in between. Think of tic-tac-toe: every X player one adds to the game brings player two closer to losing. Every O player two puts in does the same for player one. It also works on the stock exchange, where gains in the futures market depend on someone else losing.

The expression originated in game theory, a branch of applied mathematics whose influence extends to economics, international politics, and many other fields (including tic-tac-toe and the stock exchange). One of the theory's most famous exponents is the mathematician and Nobel Prize–winner John Nash and, if you think you have never heard of him, think back to the film *A Beautiful Mind*: John Nash is the character played by Russell Crowe. "Oh yes," I can hear you mumbling. "Game theory. I remember now."

4

Mushroom Management

HOW NOT TO DO IT

In the last chapter we tried to give management the benefit of the doubt. They are doing their best, gosh darn it. In this chapter all such charity is thrown out the window. These are red-flag terms that mean the bosses are getting it wrong.

Bandwagon Effect

A bandwagon is something you jump on. Originally and literally it was the wagon that carried a band of musicians during a parade. You might jump on it because it looked like so much fun that you got carried away by your enthusiasm. It sounds like something Tom Sawyer might have done, and it dates back to about that period—the late nineteenth century.

In business the bandwagon effect describes something that is done simply because others are doing it: producing gloomy thrillers set in Scandinavia, perhaps, or little tubs of yogurt that promise to lower cholesterol (only as part of a healthy diet and lifestyle, though—always read the small print).

The bandwagon effect is said to be especially influential in American politics: Someone who is rated highly in the polls will attract more votes simply because he or she is rated highly in the polls.

Blamestorming

A recent coinage and an obvious spoof on **BRAINSTORM-ING**, this is a meeting or discussion intended to establish why something went wrong. It goes without saying that all concerned are trying to avoid responsibility and blame someone else. Now that some say we aren't supposed to use "brainstorming" any more, it's tempting to wonder whether "fault showering" or "accusatory rains" might be a logical development. Or, in the legal world, perhaps "tort showering."

Checking Boxes

The idea of checking boxes derives from questionnaires and multiple-choice tests in which no original thought is required: the answers are in front of you, you merely have to pick the most appropriate (or, in the case of some magazine quizzes, the least inappropriate) one. The modern version of this is to click on the box saying, "I have read and understood the terms and conditions . . ." when everyone knows you have done no such thing.

Deriving from this comes the depressing activity familiar to many **CUBICLE MONKEYS**: going through the motions of work, being seen to do what the bosses require without actually putting any thought into it.

I Hear What You Are Saying

This remark is almost invariably followed (aloud or sotto voce) by "but I disagree with every word of it" or "I am going to ignore it entirely." The participants in this conversation are generally boss and underling, with underling objecting to some unpopular action or policy and boss digging his heels in. Speaking these words, however, enables the boss to persuade himself that he is operating an **OPEN-DOOR MANAGEMENT** policy.

I Know/See Where You're Coming From

This is capable of at least two interpretations, depending on the tone in which it is spoken. In both instances it means very little more than "I see what you mean," but this can either be filled with doubt and almost certainly followed by "but . . ." (as with **I HEAR WHAT YOU ARE SAYING**), or it can be meditative. "Hmm, I know where you're coming from" is the closest some bosses can get to "Wow, that's a good idea." Even if your proposal is then implemented and turns out to be a great success, you are advised not to hold your breath waiting to receive the credit for it.

If It Ain't Broke, Don't Fix It

We used to say "leave well enough alone," meaning don't meddle with something that is working perfectly well because you'll probably do more harm than good. "If it ain't broke, don't fix it," which means basically the same thing, is said to have been around in the rural parlance of the South for some years before it was popularized by Thomas Bertram Lance, Director of the Office of Management and Budget under President Jimmy Carter. Bert, as he was known, was quoted in a 1977 newsletter of the US Chamber of Commerce:

> Bert Lance believes he can save Uncle Sam billions if he can get the government to adopt a simple motto: "If it ain't broke, don't fix it." He explains: "That's the trouble with government: Fixing things that aren't broken and not fixing things that are broken."

In the same year, Bert was involved in a financial scandal that inspired the journalist William Safire to write a Pulitzer Prize–winning piece entitled "Carter's Broken Lance." Bert resigned soon afterward, perhaps taking the view that there was no point even attempting to fix his political career.

Micromanagement

Giving absolutely no thought to the **BIG PICTURE**, micromanagers manage every paper clip and coffee cup. Their subordinates have no opportunity to use their discretion or even just quietly do their jobs. Instead they spend a quarter of their time doing their jobs, a quarter of their time hearing about how to redo their jobs from their boss, another quarter redoing their work, and the final quarter having **WATER-COOLER TALKS** to complain about the whole damn thing. The expression has been around—and driving its victims crazy—since the 1970s.

Mushroom Management

Not normally advocated as a serious course of action, this means "keep employees in the dark and feed them bullshit." Slang supremo Jonathon Green's *Dictionary of Jargon* (1987) defines "mushroom theory" slightly differently: "a theory of management that tacitly considers that the best way of treating employees is to 'put them in the dark, feed them shit and watch them grow.'" This surely suggests that the outcome will be positive, a view most disgruntled employees living on this diet in the gloom would disagree with. The *Oxford English Dictionary*'s earliest reference is dated 1989, but refers to the "familiar philosophy of mushroom management"—and certainly the idea of disgruntled employees getting sick on bullshit has been with us since some poor minion had to drag the wooden horse inside the walls of Troy.

Nibbled to Death by Ducks

Harvard professor Stephen Walt, writing in the first six months of Barack Obama's presidency, worried that the new president's foreign policy would be met by unfulfilled promises of cooperation from various other nation states, making it very difficult to implement. The policy therefore ran the risk of failing "not because he loses some dramatic confrontation,

but simply because a whole array of weaker actors manage to grind him down. In this scenario he doesn't get vanquished, just 'nibbled to death by ducks.'"

It's a bit like **SALAMI TACTICS**. No single dreadful thing happens, but the end result is still a canceled project, a slashed budget, or constructive dismissal. Ducks don't have teeth, but they can deliver a powerful—and damaging—peck.

The earliest use of this expression I can find is in the title of a crime novel by Robert Campbell published in 1989. Mr. Campbell, an Oscar-nominated Hollywood scriptwriter as well as a novelist, had a penchant for animal-based phrases: *Nibbled to Death by Ducks* is one of a series whose other titles include *The Cat's Meow*, *The Gift Horse's Mouth*, and alarmingly, *Hip Deep in Alligators*. The fact that his publishers thought *Nibbled to Death by Ducks* was a saleable title suggests that it was an established phrase by the time he submitted his manuscript, but that theory could be eaten away by penguins if put under close scrutiny.

One-Trick Pony

Not much of business speak originates in the circus, but this is the exception to that rule. As early as 1905, a cruddy circus performer was regarded as a one-trick pony because their repertoire was limited to only one feat. In the business world, the expression has been in use since the 1990s and refers to a company that produces only one halfway-decent product or a person of limited abilities who is at a loss outside their own specialty area. You might have thought that knowing your

73

area of expertise and sticking to it would be a good thing, but not in this instance: being a one-trick pony is not going to earn you respect or a promotion but it may get you a ticket to the glue factory.

Reinventing the Wheel

This is by definition an unnecessary thing to do, as the wheel was invented at least 5,500 years ago and has worked incredibly well ever since. Yet there are always those who don't trust the work of their predecessors or colleagues and to whom the words "pragmatism" and "just get on with it" are unknown.

They waste time, effort, and resources running around in circles (appropriately enough, given what they are trying to reinvent) in order to arrive, exhausted with deadlines missed and budgets exceeded, exactly where they started. The expression has been around since the 1950s, while the concept, to the hair-tearing frustration of those who *do* understand pragmatism and getting on with it, is timeless.

Revolving-Door Policy

If you walk into a revolving door from the outside of a building and keep pushing, you quickly end up outside again. If your business is going down the tubes and you lose one CEO after another, you may be accused of having a "revolving-door policy," suggesting that the CEOs don't have time to come in and take their coats off before being escorted back out.

Revolving doors were invented in the late nineteenth century, but the term was adopted by the business world only recently—though of course the idea that CEOs don't know whether they are coming or going is as old as time.

Salami Tactics/Salami Technique

Salami tactics, perhaps surprisingly, have their origins in Hungary. Or perhaps it is not surprising on second thought, as salami features prominently in the Hungarian diet. (They spell it szalámi, but then they call food élelmiszer and pork disznóhús, so szalámi is one of their easier words.) Anyway, in the middle of the twentieth century, Hungary's ruling Communist Party was led by an unpleasant-sounding individual called Mátyás Rákosi. According to a 1952 edition of the *Times*, he described one stage in his rise to power as "'salami tactics,' by which slices of the Small-holders' Party were cut away and its strength worn down." In other words, the people of Hungary woke up one morning to find Mr. Rákosi in undisputed charge, because his removal of the opposition had been so subtle that nobody noticed what was going on until it was too late.

This softly-softly approach has been taken one stage further and developed into the salami *technique*: "a type of computer fraud in which small amounts of money are transferred from numerous customer accounts into an account held under a false name." The idea is that if you embezzle small enough amounts from enough people, again nobody will notice. Meanwhile your illicit bank balance will grow very nicely and you'll be inundated with requests from people wanting to spend their vacation in your villa on the Cayman Islands.

Trickle-Down

It may look like a verb, but trickle-down is more commonly used as a noun or an adjective (as in "trickle-down effect"). The idea is that something which benefits the higher (read: wealthier) sectors of society or a corporation will eventually benefit the poorer elements too. It's a concept that seems to have arisen in the 1930s and has since been much poohpoohed by the poorer elements who are still waiting for the trickle to reach them. As early as 1949 President Harry S. Truman dismissed the whole idea. In his State of the Union address he maintained that:

> During the last sixteen years [i.e., since his party had been in power], our people have been creating a society which offers new opportunities for every man to enjoy his share of the good things of life. We have rejected the discredited theory that the fortunes of the nation should be in the hands of a privileged few. We have abandoned the "trickle-down" concept of national prosperity. Instead, we believe that our economic system should rest on a democratic foundation and that wealth should be created for the benefit of all.

Unfortunately this concept has proved harder to dry up than Truman thought.

Waiting for the Other Shoe to Drop

In the business context, the "other shoe" normally signifies a second wave of layoffs: survivors of the first pass of the ax wait nervously to lose their own jobs and—in what has been described as "other shoe syndrome"—become so unproductive that the cost savings made by the original cutbacks are wasted. According to Eric Partridge in *A Dictionary of Catch Phrases* (1977), the expression derives from a story about a lodging house. A lodger in an upstairs room routinely dropped his shoes loudly on the floor, one after the other, every night when he went to bed. His downstairs neighbor complained, but the next night the upstairs lodger dropped the first shoe as usual. Then he remembered that he had promised not to do this any more. When he removed his other shoe, he put it down on the floor gently and quietly. After a long pause, the downstairs neighbor, who had been lying awake all this time, yelled, "For God's sake, drop the other shoe!"

Wake-Up Call

In simpler times this used to just be what you got in a hotel when you asked the clerk at the front desk to ring you at an obscenely early hour. Nowadays, you can program your cell phone to perform the same service, with a smaller chance of human error, so wake-up calls have become largely figurative. Instead of jet-lagged executives, the recipients are usually managers whose bad results should alert them to the fact that their current course or action is likely to end in disaster. In other words, wake-up calls no longer say, "Good morning, ma'am, it's 5 a.m." They say, "What did you do!? Fix it now!"

Worst-Case Scenario

It simply means "the worst thing that can happen," but that is the sort of clear, no-nonsense English that has no place in today's business world. This is now such a universally recognized phrase that many people say merely "worst case," leaving their audience to supply the rest.

The expression was popular enough in 1999 for Joshua

Piven and David Borgenicht to have a spectacular success with their *Worst-Case Scenario Survival Handbook*, which contains such invaluable advice as how to escape from quicksand, fend off a shark, deliver a baby in a taxicab, and survive if your parachute fails to open. All of these scenarios suggest that—assuming Joshua and David are writing from experience—they are running far too many unnecessary risks and should either stay at home and take it a bit easier or look very closely at their insurance policies. Or both.

5

The Way Forward

When all else fails, businesses bring in management consultants to show them what to do next. Opinions vary greatly as to how much value is delivered for the money spent on these occasions, but one thing cannot be denied: They have created a whole new vocabulary and introduced brand-new meanings to many everyday words.

Action

On the basis that "any noun can be verbed," and also that a saving of nanoseconds is of value in business speak, this has come to be preferred to "put into action" or "act upon" in contexts such as actioning tasks that need to be completed or actioning decisions that were made at a meeting. Although purists scowl and maintain that this usage is yet another sign that the world is going to hell in a handbasket, the *Oxford English Dictionary* has an example dated 1960 and another from Len Deighton's *The Ipcress File* (1962). If it's good enough for Michael Caine, it's good enough for me.

Oh no, on second thought, it isn't. It's terrible. Sorry, Sir Michael.

Bottom-Up

See **TOP-DOWN MANAGEMENT**.

Broker

As a verb, in the sense of "to broker a deal," "to act as a broker, to negotiate," this feels like another vile piece of modern jargon of the "any noun can be verbed" variety (see **ACTION**). But in fact, it was first recorded in 1638 in the UK. However, in the nineteenth century and for most of the twentieth its use was almost exclusively American. So this is a verb that originated in the UK, crossed the Atlantic, fell into disuse in its home country, and has only recently crossed back again. Perhaps the British purists have something to complain about after all. There can be no objection to the word as a noun but, according to Britain's *Chambers Dictionary*, a broker's occupation is not to broker but to broke. And, as we all know, **IF IT AIN'T BROKE, DON'T FIX IT**.

Buying Into

These days, buying into something doesn't necessarily involve parting with money. Yes, you can "buy into" a company by investing in stocks and shares, but you can also "buy into" a management ethos or a government policy without putting your hands in your pockets. All you are required to do is to believe in them wholeheartedly and embrace them without reservation. Which, of course, may end up costing you something more important than cash in the long run.

Core Competencies

Businessdictionary.com has a fifty-word definition for core competencies that includes "what give a firm one or more competitive advantages in creating and delivering value to its customers in its chosen field." But "what we're good at" sums it up.

From the same source comes the definition of "core rigidities," the "flip side" of core competencies: ". . . caused by over-reliance on any advantage(s) for too long. While a successful firm's management relaxes its improvement efforts, others keep on getting better and obsolete its competitive advantage."

I quote that largely because I have never seen "obsolete" used as a verb before, and though it's technically correct usage, I hope I never do again.

Delayering

In use since at least the 1990s, this is a specific form of **DOWN-SIZING** that involves disposing of tiers of management and simplifying the hierarchy. Delayering makes the organization less bureaucratic and the decision-making process quicker, thus giving the company a better competitive "edge." Sounds good, doesn't it? Maybe, but it is still a euphemism for people losing their jobs, which is not good even if they are mostly bureaucrats.

Delivery

Mailmen and women deliver things. (If you have a really long memory, you might recall when kids on bikes with baskets on the front used to deliver things.) Oh, those were the days. A delivery was the mail, a couple of pounds of stewing steak that you had ordered from the butcher's, maybe some fresh milk in glass bottles, or whatever. The point is that it was a physical object.

Nowadays, delivery is also known to be the means by which a service meets the END USER. An "electronic delivery strategy" is jargonista speak for a plan for making services available online. It would be wrong to poke too much fun at this usage. It's a prime example of the way a garden-variety word evolves to cope with a new invention or phenomenon. Who knew that when the paperboy rode by and tossed a paper on your doorstep, he was the analog prototype of the electronic delivery of the same paper to your tablet.

Direct Report

Why do people think that saying things in plain English makes them look unsophisticated? Yes, this is quicker than saying "someone in my department" or "someone who reports to me," but isn't it ugly? The sense of "report" meaning a human being reporting rather than a written or verbal account has not, at the time of writing, made it into the dictionaries. And long may that continue to be the case.

Dynamic

As an adjective meaning "energetic," this word has been around since the middle of the nineteenth century, having evolved from the science of dynamics, which studies

movement. As a noun meaning "an energizing force" it soon drifted away from the scientific world, so that by the late twentieth century it had come to mean first something that drove a social change ("the dynamic behind the swing to the left") then the change itself ("the new left-wing dynamic"). From there it was but a short step to management-consultant speak for how people get along, as in "His not being there changed the whole dynamic of the meeting" and "Having a few young people around changes the dynamic of the office." This sense has yet to appear in the dictionaries, but it can't be far off.

Empowerment

What is it about this word that makes the skin crawl? It's a perfectly reasonable concept, "the action of empowering; the state of being empowered." To empower someone simply means "to give somebody power for a purpose, to enable them to do something." Both words have been around for a hundred (in the case of empower, several hundred) years. But the modern definition of "giving people power to make decisions about themselves, particularly with regard to self-development" belongs with all those motivational courses that teach people to say "challenge" when they mean "problem" and encourage women to "reclaim the goddess within."

Bill Gates has spoken about empowering workers in order to make their jobs more interesting, which will in turn make them work more diligently and enthusiastically. But he was talking about giving them information that was "just a few clicks away"—in other words, keeping them (IN THE) LOOP. I don't *think* he meant that the staff of Microsoft should reclaim the goddess within, though you never know . . .

Engagement

This is a word that has had many shades of meaning in its time, all to do with agreements, arrangements, or obligations. They range from something as important as a marriage engagement to something as delicious as a dinner engagement. Two swords might be engaged in the course of a fencing match, or a craftsman could be engaged in a delicate piece of work.

Nowadays sales and marketing people are urged to engage with their customers in order to build stronger and more profitable relationships, to ensure **BRAND** loyalty, and **DELIVER** great experiences across the whole "customer life cycle." It's another form of **CUSTOMER VALUE ORIENTATION** and similarly a grand name for a fairly basic concept.

Face Time

Another instance of "my time is so important, I must save every possible fraction of a second by speaking in abbreviations that have become too short to make any sense" (see **DIRECT REPORT**). Try this exercise: If your watch is sensitive enough, time yourself saying "face time." Then time yourself saying "face-to-face time" (which is what it means), and calculate the difference. Now work out how many messages you could send on your BlackBerry in the time you have saved. Not all that many, is my guess.

Anyway, "face-to-face time" means "getting together in the same room," as opposed to communicating by phone, e-mail, or whatever. We used to call it a meeting.

Facilitator

"To facilitate" is to make something easy or easier, and it has meant that since the sixteenth century. A person who facilitates has been a facilitator since the eighteenth. The beginning of the meaning that many of us would dismiss as modern jargon—a person or organization that promotes communication or negotiation between various others, a conference organizer or coordinator—has been around since 1928. But as a fancy word for "guide" (like the bored housewife who shows you around a museum), it dates—as so many expressions in this book do—from that jargon-ridden decade, the 1980s.

Functional Flexibility

Isn't this a beautiful expression? If you have this, you are able to cover when someone else is away or when one department is more stressed than another. It translates into day-to-day English as "being able to do lots of jobs." It's not as strong as jack-of-all-trades; it's more like jack-of-all-things-in-one-trade.

Going Forward

"We'll be looking at how we can improve things going forward," said a British Airports Authority spokesman when Heathrow was in chaos after heavy snow in the days leading up to some Christmas or other (it's difficult to keep track now that this seems to be a regular feature of the Christmas season). The expression means little more than "in the future" or "from now on," with the subtle undertone of placation. To all intents and purposes it's verbal filler that could, um, be dispensed with, y'know?

Horizontal Initiative

Despite what you might think at first glance, this is no more connected with sex than **MISSIONARY SELLING**. Social commentators have been making the distinction between "horizontal" and "vertical" (usually in terms of class or wealth) for a surprisingly long time. The Russian-born American sociologist Pitirim Sorokin was writing about horizontal and vertical social mobility as early as 1927. So it is really the use of "initiative" to mean "project" or "idea" that turns this expression into jargon. This use has not yet been recognized by standard dictionaries, but it is a favorite among lovers of gobbledygook and claptrap.

In the workplace, anything "vertical" operates in the traditional direction of a manager telling a subordinate what to do and the subordinate doing it and reporting back. Working "horizontally" means involving more than one department/

agency/organization. This inevitably brings with it all the problems of liaising with others who are on an equal footing. Motivating people who are not answerable to you and may not feel the task is as important as you do; ensuring that, although it is a joint enterprise, you get the credit if it goes well; and making sure that your horizontal partners share the blame if it is a disaster can be challenging. To counterbalance these negative aspects, in a horizontal initiative you get to use other people's data and expertise—provided, of course, they can be persuaded to share it with you.

(Get) In Bed (With)

An expression, and indeed a concept, that needs to be used carefully if you don't want to find yourself making headlines in the tabloids. It means—appropriately enough—"form a

(probably casual and unofficial) partnership with," though it may also be used for a formal merger. In fact it is more like a marriage, though probably one of convenience. Although we tend to think of most business jargon as being coined in the 1970s or '80s, this gem was recorded as early as 1885.

Open-Door Management

Having a policy of "come on in, my door is always open" is supposed to encourage trust within a company. Employees believe that the boss is part of the team and that any contributions they make will be taken seriously. However, management consultants are quick to point out that a manager, who sits in their office all day, even with the door open, is no substitute for one who gets out there among the workers and has a feel for what is going on before complaints or anxieties start to fester.

Similarly, it is a foolish manager who believes that all is well just because he has had a one-on-one meeting with a subordinate who had no issues to raise. This is much more likely to mean that the subordinates don't trust the manager enough to confide in him or her. Or that their ideas have been shot down in flames once too often, so they are resigned to doing things the manager's way. It's no cakewalk for the boss either. He or she has to deal with all the personalities and problems in an office, but face it, if you are the boss, you wouldn't be getting paid so generously if it were easy.

Outsourcing

This is a glorified form of subcontracting. Although it can refer to goods, it is more frequently used for buying services from another company. Outsourcing came to prominence in the 1980s when companies were **DOWNSIZING** their permanent staff and needed freelancers to do the work no longer being done in-house. It has since been much adopted by the public sector.

Indeed outsourcing has become such a contributor to public services that one "services and outsourcing" company—which runs, among other things, various public transport services, four prisons, and a major laboratory—has a turnover of more than $5 billion. To put that into perspective, there are around forty countries in the world with lower GDPs. We're talking big business here.

Ownership

Well, obviously, we know what this means. But in the jargon context one can have "ownership" of something as large and un-ownable as the environment. It's the modern term for feeling involved and taking responsibility. In the workplace, it's about taking pride in and responsibility for your work and/or wanting the company that pays your salary to do well. Business expert Michael Bergdahl wrote of Sam Walton, founder of Wal-Mart, that he "instilled ownership of the products in the stores into the collective consciousness of every associate, regardless of what job they did for the company." Looking at the size Wal-Mart is today, you'd have to think that this worked pretty well.

Performance Coaching

There used to be management training, a wide-reaching concept whose aim was to make people better at their job. Now there is performance coaching, whose aim is fundamentally the same. Perhaps the first half of "management training" sounded too elitist and the second too prescriptive. In the twenty-first century we are more into personal development and **EMPOWERMENT** than into explicitly telling people what to do.

Proactive

"Tending to initiate change rather than reacting to events;" in other words a **SELF-STARTER**, someone who can come up with ideas and act on them without waiting for someone else to tell them what to do.

The word has its origins in psychology and psychiatry, where it is first recorded in the 1930s. It had moved into more general parlance by the 1960s and been coopted by business speak by the 1980s. Today it's made its way into everyday speech, thanks to Jessica Simpson advocating acne medication.

Quality-Driven

See **RESULTS-DRIVEN**.

Rationalizing

The most recent definition of "rationalize," and the one that is most relevant to us, is "to organize (an industry) so as to achieve greater efficiency and economy." That is *The Chambers Dictionary* at its elegant best—it carefully makes no mention of firing people, although that is implicit.

Since the seventeenth century "rationalize" has meant "to explain, to make reasonable," and since the eighteenth Rationalism has been a philosophical concept that helps to explain (or explain away) God. In the early twentieth century psychologists started using "rationalizing" to describe the way patients justified their *un*reasonable behavior to themselves and others with what the *Oxford English Dictionary* winningly describes as "plausible but specious reasons."

It was about that time—the 1920s—that economists adopted the term to describe the reorganization of a business in order to avoid wastage of time, labor, or materials. As early as this (it was the decade of the stock market crash and birth of the Great Depression) it implied specifically making cuts, reducing numbers of employees, or closing down parts of a business in order to make the rest run more efficiently. In those early days, though, you rationalized a business, a department, a system; nowadays the concept is so clearly understood that the verb can be used intransitively. If you say, "They are rationalizing in Washington," no one is going to ask, "Rationalizing what?"

Resource Allocation

A fancy-schmancy expression for "how you spend your money." There are systems and matrixes and models to help you do it, but that is what it boils down to.

Results-Driven

It has long been an axiom among journalists of the better sort that the way to test if an expression is redundant or plain nonsense is to consider its opposite. For example, the fact that you can't have a dangerous haven or a wonderful disaster makes a mockery of "safe haven" or "terrible disaster." In the same spirit, in their splendid book *Why Business People Speak Like Idiots: a Bullfighter's Guide* (2005), Brian Fugere, Chelsea Hardaway, and Jon Warshawsky give the opposite of "results-driven" as "for the sheer hell of it." They point out that, as so few business proposals have succeeded with "for the sheer hell of it" as their declared motivation, "results-driven" is a good expression to drop from corporate vocabulary. By the same token, describing your business as "quality-driven" becomes valid only if your competitors have come out and admitted that they deliberately produce garbage.

Revenue Stream

This is an expression with a wide variety of uses, all of them to a greater or lesser extent pretentious. Dating from the 1920s—which is surprising for something that sounds so obviously like modern jargon—it can be used in the stock market, where assets may be said to have "a future revenue stream," i.e., we can sell 'em later and make money. Governments have used "revenue stream" because it sounds better than "income generated by taxes." In business it means little more than "sales."

Increasingly, however, it has come to mean "a new and exciting source of income"—the Kindle is a new revenue stream for Amazon, for example, or podcasting may be a revenue stream for a radio station. As long as the cash keeps flowing in, though, it doesn't much matter what you call it.

Skill Set

This is a neologism for "things you can do." The important part of this is really the "set." Some of the attributes of an accomplished diplomat, for example, might be linguistic ability, tact, shrewdness, and an awareness of the differences between various cultures. Put them all together and you have a skill set. (See also **KNOWLEDGE BASE**.)

Stakeholders

The earliest (eighteenth-century) stakeholders were the guys who saw that there was fair play in betting games, but the "modern" sense of "someone with a financial or other interest in the success of an organization" is almost as old, recorded first in the 1820s. Nevertheless, it has the stigma of recent jargon about it, enabling the writers of reports to produce statements such as:

> The business models set out below take into account the stakeholders involved and our understanding of their needs and priorities . . . The interests of the various stakeholders are not always well aligned, meaning that there may need to be winners and losers to make some of these business models viable.

In this context, the word means little more than "people involved" and is one of those mystifying terms employed by those who have a rooted objection to the use of plain English.

Then there is that mysterious entity, the stakeholder pension. A government website helpfully explains to the bemused buyer that "stakeholder pensions are a type of personal pension" and that "stakeholder pensions work in much the same way as other money purchase pensions." Confusion gone mad.

SWOT Analysis

SWOT stands for strengths, weaknesses, opportunities, and threats. A SWOT analysis is a game played in conference rooms up and down the land when the person in charge of stationery has accidentally ordered ten years' worth of Post-it Notes, and they need to be used up in order to make room for other stuff in the supply closet.

The idea is that a group of employees gets together to

consider the business, its competitors, and the state of the market. You need four whiteboards or flip-charts (labeled S, W, O, and T) and a supply of Post-it Notes. Each person writes down any strengths, weaknesses, opportunities, and threats they can think of, each on a separate Post-it. These are then stuck to the relevant board, and you all gather around to read each other's contributions. With any luck, before this has bored you to sleep it will be time to take the plastic wrap off the trays of sandwiches thoughtfully provided by the marketing manager. Once you've eaten those, it should be time to go back to work. If not, you may be able to fit in a quick round of Pin the Tail on the Donkey.

Management consultant Albert Humphrey is said to have invented SWOT analysis in the 1960s. It was initially called SOFT analysis, with the F standing for "fault." Perhaps that was a little too soft for the concrete jungle, so it was changed to something that was more likely to invoke thoughts of the SWAT team instead of a comfy pillow.

Top-Down Management

Given that this means "management telling underlings what to do," you may think that this is just the way life is and wonder if we need a term for it. Well, apparently so, because top-down management is not as popular as it used to be. Except, it seems, when it is crucial to get things done. The rest of the time, when presumably it doesn't matter whether things get done or not, "team-based management" is the in thing and is defined as "an approach that **PROACTIVE**ly seeks the

input of multiple **STAKEHOLDERS** in the decision-making process," which seems to combine all the best elements of inde-
cisiveness and saying, "Well, gee, I'm not sure. What do you
think?" It is also known as "engaging multiple perspectives
within the company."

Team-based management may also take a "bottom-up"
approach, which sadly means it will listen to ideas from the
lower echelons instead of meaning something fun, like an
alternative to "Cheers" when raising a glass. See **MISSION-
ARY SELLING** for something else that isn't as interesting as it
sounds.

Transparency

This word became a big deal after the Enron scandal and the
ensuing crash and burn of the economy in 2008. Having
transparency is supposed to restore the public's faith in companies that are too big to fail. It is also something the government is supposed to have to restore the public's faith in the
bailouts for the companies that are too big to fail. Hmm.

However, "transparency" as a guard against corruption
is not a new concept. Transparency International, the self-
styled "global coalition against corruption," has for fifteen
years been preparing an annual Corruption Perceptions Index
which measures the perceived corruption of 178 nations on a
scale of 0 (unbelievably corrupt) to 10 (equally unbelievably
squeaky clean). Somalia, Afghanistan, and Myanmar were
2010's lowest scorers, which is a sad reflection on the state
of the world.

As a matter of interest, the only countries scoring 9 or more ("practically perfect in every way") were Denmark, New Zealand, and Singapore (all on 9.3), and Finland and Sweden (both 9.2). Canada was sixth with 8.9, Australia eighth with 8.7, the UK twentieth with 7.6, and the US twenty-second, equal with Belgium at 7.1.

(The) Way Forward

This is politician speak for "the best thing to do," but somehow it sounds more positive and gives the impression that the speaker has given the matter some thought. Hearers are invited (by me, not necessarily by the politicians) to draw their own conclusions.

Window of Opportunity

The point of a window of opportunity is that it occupies a small, limited area or time frame and should be grasped quickly before it slips away. An early (1980) example refers to the US/USSR arms race, when the Soviets had a "window of opportunity" to knock out some American missiles. They didn't react quickly enough, and the moment passed.

From this confrontational beginning, the expression was taken up by proponents of **EMPOWERMENT** and became an inspirational cliché meaning little more than "opportunity" in contexts such as, "Life's ups and downs provide windows of opportunity to determine what is important to you. Think of

them as stepping stones that will help you reach your goals."

In the modern workplace, however, a window of opportunity (or just a window) has come to be a synonym for "a free moment in my schedule." It is used by people who think they are busier and more important than you are, but you would probably be well-advised to smother your irritation and arrange a meeting (or "set up some FACE TIME") with them while you have the chance.

6

KSF in FMCG

ABBREVIATIONS AND ACRONYMS

TLAs—three-letter acronyms—are all the rage in the business world, but some are so cumbersome that you wonder why we bother. The prime example of this is WWW, which takes a lot longer to say than "worldwide web," so it has largely been ditched in favor of the less tongue-twisting "web."

B2B

Even those who rail against everything possible being abbreviated these days will admit that "business to business" is a bit of a mouthful after a decent lunch. They'd also find it hard to deny that, although the introduction of the 2 is both inaccurate, BtoB would have been a terrible acronym.

The point of B2B is that it involves two businesses rather than a business and a consumer, as this 1998 quote from the *Financial Times* makes clear: "These potential **REVENUE STREAMS** present growth opportunities for incumbents and a fresh **PARADIGM** for new entrants, both of which feel compelled to embrace B2B (business-to-business) in order to succeed." When I say "clear," I mean, of course, "as mud."

BCP/BPCP

See **DRP**.

BOGOF

A prime example of the power of **PULL MARKETING**, this is an ugly-sounding acronym for what most people think of as an attractive concept—"buy one, get one free." BOGOHP (". . . get one half price") is another familiar ploy, but for some reason it hasn't passed into the language as an acronym. The abbreviation BOGOF has been around for a quarter of a century but has been used with increasing frequency in recent years as retailers have become more and more desperate for our business. It's now not unusual to see it as bogof, without explanation or capital letters—so that, as with radar and scuba, we'll soon be forgetting that it was ever an acronym at all.

DRP

This concept of disaster recovery planning is probably best defined by the subtitle of the bible on the subject by American

IT consultant Jon William Toigo: *Preparing for the Unthinkable*.

The point of DRP—also known as BCP or BPCP (business continuity plan or business process contingency plan)—is that if you plan ahead thoroughly enough, you will be prepared even if the absolute worst happens. The effects of a disaster will be minimized and normal service will be resumed as soon as possible. As IT systems become ever more complex, of course, there are more and more things that can go wrong, and in order to be of any use at all, disaster recovery plans have to be ever more sophisticated. Standing in the parking lot drying circuit boards with a hair dryer just doesn't cut it any more.

Mr. Toigo has been preaching his message for twenty years, but his disaster recovery site reports limited **PENETRATION**: "Despite the number of very public disasters since 9/11, still only about 50 percent of companies report having a disaster recovery plan. Of those that do, nearly half have never tested their plan, which is tantamount to not having one at all." A worrying thought, suggesting that most emergency plans just consist of **FIRE-FIGHTING**.

ETA

An extraordinarily versatile—some might say dangerously ambiguous—abbreviation whose meaning depends entirely on where and who you are and what you are doing. If you're traveling, it could be either estimated time of arrival (an expression that dates back to World War II) or Electronic Travel Authority, an alternative to a visa for entry into Australia (much more recent). If you're in charge of an oil tanker, it is likely to be emergency towing arrangement. In the IT world it could be embedded transport acceleration, developed by Intel with a view to speeding up communication between servers. A stargazer may translate it as extraterrestrial activity. For a Basque separatist it is the name of a political party, although in Spanish it is also an abbreviation for automated weather stations. In Portugal it is short for "I love you."

In other words, be careful how you use it. Particularly in Portugal.

FMCG

The website www.fmcg.co.uk (yes, there really is such a thing) defines fast-moving consumer goods as "simply

the essential items that one must have in order to live—or at least live well." The most obvious FMCGs are items that leave the supermarket shelves quickly, things that most people buy most weeks. However, you don't have to go to the supermarket to buy FMCGs. They can be delivered to your home, or they can include something you might pick up from a convenience store, a pharmacy, or a "tobacco or smoking paraphernalia store." Stationery, candy, and booze are also FMCGs.

The point of fast-moving consumer goods is, from the customer's point of view, that they are cheap and have a short life expectancy; as far as manufacturers and retailers are concerned, margins may be low but the goods sell in sufficiently high volume for the overall profit to be substantial. The opposite of an FMCG is a consumer durable, such as a washing machine, which is expensive, lasts a long time, and is bought in small quantities, but has a higher profit margin on each item. It isn't usually referred to as a CD, for the simple reason that the inventors of compact discs got there first.

FPO

See **IPO**.

FUD

Fear, uncertainty, and doubt are three closely related negative feelings deliberately planted in the minds of the public by those involved in marketing, PR, politics, and other **SPIN**-related disciplines. FUD-spreaders tend to belong to the big companies, the major parties, and the mainstream in general. Their aim is to make their customers or voters scared to buy a new product or vote for an unproven party. Computing entrepreneur Gene Amdahl left IBM to set up the company that bears his name in the 1970s and accused his former employer of instilling FUD in the minds of potential customers for Amdahl products. He may have invented—and he certainly popularized—the acronym, but the concept had been around for at least half a century before he used it.

Opponents of FUD have used terms such as "implicit coercion" and "disinformation" with reference to computer giants and others. They have also found themselves in court as a result, so let's leave it there.

If by any chance you pursue wildfowl shooting as a hobby, particularly in Australia, you may think that FUD stands for "fold-up decoy"—a flat-pack version of a decoy used in pursuit of ducks, geese and pigeons. If so, I'm afraid you may somehow have strayed into the wrong book.

IPO

An initial public offering is the first offering of stock for sale to the public by a private company. According to the website investopedia.com, IPOs are often issued by small companies seeking the capital to expand, but sometimes also by large privately owned companies looking to become publicly traded. The site goes on to advise that:

... IPOs can be a risky investment. For the individual investor, it is tough to predict what the stock will do on its initial day of trading and in the near future because there is often little historical data with which to analyze the company. Also, most IPOs are of companies going through a transitory growth period, which are subject to additional uncertainty regarding their future values.

There are of course exceptions to this, such as when Facebook went public, but good luck getting in on that IPO. But generally, if you're looking for a secure investment, it may be prudent to wait for an FPO (follow-on public offering), a supplementary issue of shares made once a company is established on a stock exchange.

KPI

Key performance indicators must be measurable (there's a lot of that going on in business speak: see **DASHBOARD**). And—clue in the title—they have to be key to an organization's performance. As one management website puts it, "Once an organization has analyzed its **MISSION** and defined its goals, it needs a way to measure progress towards those goals. Key Performance Indicators are these measurements." Goals can be nebulous; KPIs can't. So a goal could be "to be the most popular company in our field," but a KPI would have to include something like the percentage of first-time customers coming back for more.

What form KPIs take obviously depends on the nature of your business. If you are running a bus company, for example, one indicator might be the percentage of buses that arrive on time; or if you are in a customer-service department, it might be the percentage of calls answered within five rings. Handy hint: If it's got a number in it, it's got a fighting chance of being a KPI. If not, it is more likely to be a goal or a mission or one of the three wishes that the genie granted you.

KSFS

Key success factors in marketing speak are the factors (they are almost always plural) that are necessary for a company to succeed in a given market. If you know the two or three things that you absolutely have to be good at, and are good at them, you can get away with being mediocre at everything else. A comforting thought for the mediocrities among us.

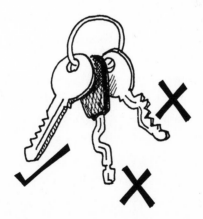

MBWA

Management consultants Tom Peters and Robert H. Waterman Jr. made the concept of "management by wandering around" famous in their 1982 book *In Search of Excellence*, reckoned by those in the know to be one of the best business books of the century. The idea was to make senior management visible and available to employees, to show that the boss was interested in how everyone was doing and was responsive to any suggestions they had to make. One website—not connected with Peters or Waterman—offers ten top tips to assist the would-be MBWA'er, but spoils the effect by including "Make certain your visits are spontaneous and unplanned." See also the less **PROACTIVE** but still well-intentioned **OPEN-DOOR MANAGEMENT.**

OEM

There are some strange acronyms and abbreviations around in the modern world, but this is one of the strangest. How, you may well ask, did OEM come to stand for "intermediate user"?

It started out sensibly enough, as an abbreviation for Original Equipment Manufacturer. An Original Equipment Manufacturer manufactures a product. Say, a washing machine. So far so good. Then the OEM sells that washing machine to a retailer to be sold under its "own brand" label. The OEM and the retailer make money, the customer has clean clothes, everyone is happy.

But let's imagine that the product isn't something finished, like a washing machine, but a computer component. The company that purchases it from the OEM isn't the retailer but an intermediary whose task is to incorporate the component into the finished item and *then* sell it on. From the retailer's point of view, it's all the same thing—he's buying a product and it doesn't matter whether the supplier is the originator or not. So that intermediary also becomes an OEM to simplify the coding on the retailer's paperwork. As far as the intermediary is concerned, the retailer is the customer, the customer is always right, so logic goes out the window and an OEM becomes an intermediate user. QED, some might say. And see also **VAR**.

RBM

Results-based management has been defined as "a management strategy by which an organization ensures that its processes, products, and services contribute to the achievement of desired results (outputs, outcomes, and impacts)." The planning process which is integral to this form of management "starts with defining objectives—deciding what accomplishments are expected if the objective is to be achieved, determining which output will lead to those accomplishments, defining the activities necessary to produce those outputs, and finally, identifying the inputs that are necessary to carry out the activities."

It all sounds very sensible, if a bit long-winded, but it makes you wonder what the opposite is: MIUAWGAASWH? Which stands for "making it up as we go along and seeing what happens." I can see that it isn't as snappy-sounding as it needs to be, so perhaps that's why it hasn't caught on with the jargonistas. See also **RESULTS-DRIVEN**.

SMB

Do we need a formal abbreviation for "small and medium-sized businesses?" Apparently so, though if we prefer not to confuse them with the San Miguel Beermen (a Filipino basketball team), a System Management Bus, a Server Message Block (both computing terms too complicated to go into here), or the Spartan Marching Band of Michigan State University, we can call them SMEs ("small and medium-sized enterprises") instead. However, we then run the risk of confusing them with the Society of Manufacturing Engineers, a NASA satellite called the Solar Mesosphere Explorer, and an economic model known as Social Market Economy. A bit like **ETA**, these are abbreviations that need to be used with care. The issue is also complicated by the fact that different countries define "small" and "medium" in different ways. What is considered small in Canada (fewer than a hundred employees in some industries) would be quite a decent size in New Zealand, for example. But then if you look at a map you can imagine that the same would be true of a number of things in those two countries.

Anyway, many governments and multinational organizations such as the European Commission, give state aid, grants for research and development, etc., to small and medium-sized businesses, so they have to be able to define them. And, having just typed small and medium-sized businesses/enterprises a number of times in the space of this entry, I can see why they decided it did indeed need to be abbreviated.

USP

Meaning "unique selling point" or "unique selling proposition," this has been the mantra of anyone involved in marketing since 1958. The three rules for a USP were defined in that year by advertising guru Rosser Reeves, the man who came up with the line "Melts in your mouth, not in your hands" to sell M&Ms. "First," he said, "you need a definite proposition. Then, second, it must be a unique proposition. Third,

the proposition must sell." Like so many ideas with which we have all grown up, it seems obvious now, but it was revolutionary at the time.

VAR

Short for value-added reseller, this refers to a company, probably in the computer world, that buys in a product from another company, adds "value" to it, perhaps by introducing its own software, and moves it on at a higher price. If what is being supplied is a service rather than a product, it may be described as a VAS (whose meaning you can probably figure out for yourself). This may, for example, enable users of cell phones to log on to the Internet, play video games, and do all sorts of other things above and beyond making phone calls. "Value added" is frequently used on its own as a noun to indicate "the amount of value that is added" at each stage of an item's production. It could have been called "added value," but that wouldn't have won it a place in economics jargon.

WOMBAT

An acronym born of the "get it all into 140 characters" culture, this is variously translated as "waste of money, brains, and time" or ". . . and talent." Whether or not it stands the test of time remains to be seen but, like many such coinages, it is kind of cute.

WYSIWYG

What you see is what you get. Originally (in the 1980s) this meant that what you saw on your computer screen was exactly what you would got on a printout—an important concept in the days when the difference between screen fonts and printer fonts caused many a nightmare for those involved in graphic design. Tending to fall into disuse in its original sense, the longer form of this acronym is sometimes used as a set phrase in a social context. Someone who doesn't bother to dress up for formal occasions or isn't renowned for the polish of his manners might, with a sense of inverted snobbery, may describe himself as a what-you-see-is-what-you-get sort of guy. If you are the host, you are under no obligation to invite this person again.

7

Creative Accounting

MONEY: ITS USES AND ABUSES

When all is said and done, it's a business. People are in it for the money. Not all of them are dishonest, but just as somebody once wondered why the devil should have all the best tunes, so you might similarly ask why the swindlers have the most imaginative turns of phrase.

Anti-Trust

This makes sense only if you are aware of a specific definition of trust: "a group of commercial enterprises combined to monopolize and control the market for any commodity: illegal in the US." Thus there are anti-trust laws that prohibit that sort of thing from happening.

Anti-trust legislation has been around for over a hundred years, but when the expression started to crop up in the news—and until we became accustomed to it—it appeared strange to those of us brought up to think that trust was a good thing.

Asset-Stripping

With no ancestry other than in the business world, this expression emerged in the 1970s to describe the action of stripping off bits of a company you had just taken over in order to make a quick profit. The implication is that you—the purchaser—were after only one thing, which in this instance wasn't sex. Say, for example, you bought the Louvre because you longed to own the Mona Lisa, and then dispersed all the Botticellis and Titians to the highest bidder. There aren't many people in the art world who wouldn't call you a Philistine, though of course with all that money and your favorite painting over the fireplace you might not care a great deal.

Ballpark

A ballpark used to be a stadium where baseball was played. It still is. Then, during World War II, it came to mean any area roughly the size of a ballpark. Later, in the early years of space exploration, it was specifically the area within which the capsule from a satellite returning to Earth was supposed to land. Next it evolved the figurative sense of any general area, so that a financial offer might not be quite as much as the vendor wanted but was "in the right ballpark"—that is, not ludicrously low and with a bit of negotiation a deal could likely be struck. From this use, it developed into today's adjective, so that we have "a ballpark figure" (not unlike a "back of the envelope figure"), meaning "an educated guess, something to work with while waiting for someone to do the math properly." First recorded in 1960, a ballpark figure is a newer concept than a guesstimate, but not necessarily a more accurate one.

As a noun, a ballpark can also be "an area of expertise," as in "I am not qualified to express an opinion; this is not my ballpark"—though if you chose to learn more about that sphere of activity you could find yourself in a whole new ballgame.

Black-Box Accounting

The term "black box"—which to most of us means the thing that helps experts find out why an airplane has crashed—is used in computing and engineering to mean a self-contained

unit whose workings need not be understood by the user. In the accounting world, it is more or less synonymous with a black hole—a place into which numbers vanish without a trace or from which they appear as if by magic.

This concept entered public awareness at the time of the Enron scandal in 2001 and is defined (by investorwords .com) as "complex and confusing accounting **METHODOLOGY** that makes financial statements hard to interpret by an untrained individual." Enron used it to manipulate its share price and disguise the fact that the company had no assets. Shareholders eventually lost some $11 billion and a number of those responsible went to jail. If the **CREATIVE ACCOUNTING** used in *The Producers* rendered the offenders "incredibly guilty," what was happening at Enron really does defy belief.

Black Friday

A "black" day is traditionally one on which disaster strikes. There was a Black Monday in October 1987 when stock markets around the world crashed; and the Wall Street crash of 1929 is called Black Tuesday. Politically incorrect it may be, in this context black = bad.

There is a bright side to black days, though. Black Friday, as in the day after Thanksgiving, gets its name from "going into the black." Retailers expect their businesses to start making a profit on that day because so many people take this unofficial holiday off to start their Christmas shopping. Retailers are happy to facilitate this modern holiday with blowout sales that get shoppers out of bed at three a.m., even after an intensive day of eating and drinking. In the last few years the marketing people have also created Cyber Monday, the Monday following Black Friday, when massive discounts are offered to encourage people to shop online. Whether you choose to do battle with the Main Street crowds or stay home in front of the computer, it's all about somebody out there finding a way to take your money.

Bottom Line

This used to mean the figure at the bottom of a financial statement indicating whether or not the company had made money. From there, starting in the 1960s, it expanded to cover a result or outcome of more or less any description. For example, "The bottom line is that they decided to get married in Vegas." Having lost any grip on its etymology, the phrase is now often used as a stand-alone to mean something like "to make a long story short" or "when you get right down to it" as in "So, bottom line, if the weather doesn't improve, I won't make it to the airport on time."

Cash Cow

An expression that has been around since the 1970s, a cash cow is a part of a business that you can *milk* (oh, yes, there is a method to some of this madness) to provide a steady source of income. It also has the advantage of requiring little investment or maintenance. The danger is that you become

impatient with the plodding, cud-chewing nature of your cow and, in an effort to make it produce faster profits, you try to turn it into the goose that laid the golden egg. Which is either a horrible mixed metaphor or a dystopian vision of a future in which cloning has gone mad. Or both.

Cost Driver

This is marketing speak for "anything that effects the cost." Cost drivers may include the cost of raw materials; economies of scale (the output of lots so that each individual one is cheaper); the importance of fixed versus variable costs (you can't get out of paying rent on the factory, but perhaps you can save on advertising); the number of links there are in your **SUPPLY CHAIN**, and how much profit each needs to make, etc. Understanding cost drivers is a key factor in a successful business. You don't need to be Bill Gates to see that knowing how much your product is going to cost goes a long way toward helping you work out your likely profits. After that, all you have to do is predict how many you are going to sell. See **CONSUMER BACKLASH**, **CONSUMER CONFIDENCE**, and **CUSTOMER VALUE ORIENTATION** for factors that may have an impact there.

Creative Accounting

The *Oxford English Dictionary* defines this as "the modification of accounts to achieve a desired end; falsification of accounts that is misleading but not necessarily illegal." It also quotes Mel Brooks's screenplay for *The Producers* (1967), in which a theatrical producer's books are comprehensively cooked so that he stands to make more money from a flop than from a hit. When, in this film, the producer is finally taken to court, the jury finds him "incredibly guilty," suggesting that in describing the practice as "not necessarily illegal," the *Oxford English Dictionary* takes a more lenient view than many of us might—especially if we were on the receiving end of it.

Dead-Cat Bounce

This expression arose in the stock markets of Singapore and Malaysia and was adopted by Wall Street in the mid-1980s.

On the basis that "even a dead cat will bounce if it is dropped from a great height," it is used to describe a brief upturn in the value of a particular stock or of a stock market in general, after it has hit rock bottom. But the emphasis is on the "brief." A dead cat, having bounced, will in due course just **HIT THE GROUND** again—and it won't be running. See also **DON'T FIGHT THE TAPE** for advice on what not to do at the time of an upturn.

Done Deal

This is shorthand for "a deal that has been done," but there's something faintly defiant about it. The subtext is often "Don't argue with me, it's too late to change it now." Alternatively, there may be an element of subterfuge, a suggestion that, although discussions are being held, they are token and the decision has already been made. Or, a third type of nuance, someone involved is being presumptuous or premature: "He's behaving as if it were a done deal [but it may yet fall through]." Origin? Like so many of the terms in this book, it was born in the US, late 1970s or thereabouts.

Double-Dip

Referring to a recession, this is the kind that makes a bit of a recovery, then thinks better of it and goes back into recession. Much in the news at the time of writing—and who knows where it will end?

A double-dip recession is not to be confused with the wonderful concept of double-dipping—that is, retiring from the military, taking a pension, then accepting a "consultancy" role with the government which in the fullness of time brings with it another pension. The reference here is not to the rollercoaster effect of a recession, but to dipping twice into an ice-cream tub to come up with two scoops.

Due Diligence

This started out as a self-explanatory legal term meaning the amount of care that was necessary in any given set of circumstances. From this it developed (in the 1960s, but used with increasing frequency in the last decade or so) into an appraisal of a company, undertaken by or on behalf of someone considering taking it over, to assess whether or not it was a shrewd investment. So from being a description of an investigation ("X carried out the investigation into Y with due diligence") it has become the investigation itself ("X carried out a due diligence into Y"). It can be only a matter of time before the original meaning is so far forgotten that it will be possible to carry out a due diligence carelessly.

Leverage

When Archimedes said, "Give me but one firm spot on which to stand and I shall move the earth," he was talking about leverage. With a long enough lever tucked under the South

Pole at one end and enough force applied to the other, he could lift up the globe.

In this literal sense the word has been around for hundreds of years, but it acquired its figurative meaning of "increased advantage or power" surprisingly early: future British Prime Minister William Gladstone was using it in 1858. Now it is (all too frequently, some would say) adopted as a jargonesque alternative to "power," particularly "buying power," as in "the large chains have more leverage than the independent outlets."

There is also a specific financial sense, in existence since the 1930s. "To leverage" means "to invest borrowed capital in the hope of making profits that will more than cover the interest you have to pay on the loan" and thus to gain control of something that you couldn't afford to buy if you used your own money. The expression has often been applied to a management buyout, fending off a hostile takeover bid with borrowed capital. In this instance, the person lending the money might be described as a **WHITE KNIGHT**.

License to Print Money

In the twenty-first century, most countries have a central bank that prints their only legal bank notes. These banks regulate the amount of money in circulation as a means of controlling inflation. You can't just keep printing cash— apparently it doesn't work that way. But obviously if you *could* print your own money (and not have the police banging on your door and hauling you off to jail as a result) you would

soon become immensely rich. Or, to turn it around the other way, if you were in possession of something immensely lucrative, you would have a metaphorical license to print money.

Opinions vary as to when the expression was coined, as it were. It is often attributed to the Canadian media baron Lord Thomson of Fleet, with reference to his ownership of Scottish Television, a newborn commercial channel, in the 1950s. He certainly said it, but there is evidence that it had been used in the US ten years earlier. Perhaps it is such an appealing concept that it independently tickled the fancy of more than one entrepreneur.

Life Cycle Cost Assessment

In the old days, a life cycle wasn't something you could assess for cost: it simply happened. The life cycle of a butterfly, for example, was egg, caterpillar, chrysalis, butterfly, with the butterfly then laying more eggs and the process beginning again. But around the 1960s the butterfly spread its wings and moved into economics, sociology, business, and in due course, the environmental movement.

Life cycle cost assessment considers not just the purchase price of an item, but what it has already cost to develop, what it will cost to keep running, and eventually what it will cost (financially and environmentally) to dispose of it. The environmental aspect has, not surprisingly, become more important in recent decades: life cycle analysis, assessment, and inventory, also known as cradle-to-the-grave analysis, are common terms in the eco-conscious part of the industrial world. They all assess the energy-consuming or pollution-producing effects of manufacturing a product, transporting it wherever it needs to go, using it until it falls apart, and then recycling it or carting it off to a landfill. Buy local and bio-degradable is the message.

Lipstick Index/Lipstick Indicator

Leonard Lauder, son of Estée and chairman of the cosmetics company that bears her name, coined this term during the recession in the first years of this century. His theory was that in a period of economic uncertainty, when a woman may feel guilty about splurging on new shoes or a purse, she compensates by indulging in smaller treats such as lipstick. Increased sales of lipstick, therefore, could be a sign of poor economic health. Economists don't really believe this, but then again most of them are men.

Ponzi Scheme

Formerly known as a bubble (from its extreme burstability) and made famous in recent years by the disgraced financier Bernie Madoff, a Ponzi scheme is a scam that lures in investors by promising high and rapid returns. The problem is that there is no company making profits at the heart of the scheme. Investor A receives dividends or profits from money put in by investor B, who in turn needs there to be an investor C if he is to have any return on his own capital. As long as there are enough investors, it doesn't matter that there are no genuine profits, but sooner or later the whole thing tends to blow up in someone's face.

The name honors, if that is the right word, Charles Ponzi (1882–1949), who became a millionaire on the back of a dodgy business involving postal reply coupons (the ones that you sent instead of a stamped addressed envelope if you were dealing with someone overseas). The sums of money involved were mind-boggling, and when it all fell apart, no fewer than six banks collapsed as a result. Ponzi was in and out of jail for the next fifteen years and his life ended in poverty. But hey, he said in not quite so many words, it was fun while it lasted.

White Knight

The White Knight in Lewis Carroll's *Through the Looking-Glass* (1872) means well but doesn't have much of a clue. He is constantly falling off his horse and doesn't realize that keeping a box upside down without closing the lid means everything in it will fall out. In the years following the book's publication "white knight" came to be used for all sorts of people who fought corruption or rescued damsels in distress, although they were generally more enthusiastic than proficient. By about 1980, the term had taken on a specific meaning on the stock exchange and the suggestion of ineptitude had been lost: a white knight is someone who comes to the rescue of a company facing a hostile takeover bid. (See also **LEVERAGE**.)

8

At the Click of a Mouse

INFORMATION TECHNOLOGY
AND THE WEB

Since the world went electronic, all sorts of concepts that would have baffled our grandparents have become commonplace, and if we are to talk about them, they need to have names. This chapter can do no more than scratch the surface of the expressions that have come into being, or been given a new lease of life, in the computer age.

Agile Development

Coined in the 2001 *Manifesto for Agile Software Development*, this means developing software that works, suits customer needs, and can respond to change rather than rigidly following a plan. Or, as the Wikipedia entry prefers to put it, "Agile software development is a group of software development **METHODOLOGIES** based on iterative and incremental development, where requirements and solutions evolve through collaboration between self-organizing, cross-functional teams." While the concept seems entirely commendable, there is something about an explanation containing no fewer than five business-speak clichés in a single sentence that makes one wonder how much it really focuses on customer needs.

(At the) Click of a Mouse

Once upon a time, and it seems a very long time ago now, we were exhorted to buy things that worked "at the touch of a button." Gone were the days of slaving over a tub and then a hot mangle in order to wash and dry clothes; the new electric washer-dryer accomplished the same task "at the touch of a button." That was all very well and good until the stupid thing broke down and left you—and your downstairs neighbors— ankle-deep in rapidly cooling gray water.

Now anything you could possibly want to buy, from vacations to theater tickets to a **STATE-OF-THE-ART** version of that same washer-dryer, is available "at the click of a mouse."

Except, of course, that it isn't. It is, at a conservative estimate, available at twenty-seven clicks of the mouse. You click to choose your own seats, click to add a hotel, rent a car, opt for the dining plan, refuse turn down service, and so on for at least twenty minutes. You click to use the same credit card as you used last time and click again to have your tickets delivered to the same address as they are always delivered to—provided, of course, that that is the address to which your credit card bills are sent.

Sorry, I was just getting into this when an error occurred in the application. Please contact support. Thank you for your patience and understanding.

The *Oxford English Dictionary* defines the adjective "one-click" as "relating to or designating a computer operation performed with one click of a mouse button" and dates it to 1985. Ah, those were younger and simpler days.

Closure

This is a word with a long and varied history. Its earliest uses (a fence or enclosure, now obsolete) date back to the fourteenth and fifteenth centuries, and even the most literal current sense (the act of closing) is seventeenth century. Shakespeare used it in the sense of "bringing something to an end." So, in a pinch, if someone scoffed at your business jargon when you were boasting about "the closure of a deal" you could claim that you were emulating Shakespeare. In a pinch.

"Closure" has additional technical applications in phonetics and geology, and in the 1920s it was adopted by Gestalt psychologists to refer to the human tendency to see an incomplete figure such as a circle with a gap in it as more complete than it is. It is probably from this usage that we developed the originally psychoanalytical and now merely psychobabblical sense of "a feeling that an emotionally difficult experience has been dealt with and can be considered to be in the past."

In the IT world, however, the word has gone off at a tangent of its own. In programming languages, according to wordiq.com, a closure is "an abstraction representing a function, plus the lexical environment . . . in which the function was created, and its application to arguments. A closure results in a fully closed term: one with no free variables left."

The term was defined in the 1960s by computer scientist Peter Landin, and I am sure we would all be very grateful if we had any idea what it meant.

Cloud-Based

In computing terms, this means "on a server" or "on the Internet" and is used for software that is downloaded each time it is used, rather than being stored on a particular piece of hardware. It allows purveyors of apps, e-books, and the like

to offer "anywhere, anytime" services. It may sound like what the old-fashioned among us call "in the ether," but at the time of writing it is being viewed as the Next Big Thing. Given the speed at which these things develop, that probably means it will be passé by the time this book is published, but what can you do?

Wikipedia tells us that cloud computing has "skyrocketed" in recent years, an odd piece of imagery which just adds to that eerie feeling of "it's out there somewhere and Big Brother is probably watching it."

Cyberspace

"Cyber" comes from the Greek meaning "to steer" and its earliest appearance in modern English was in cybernetics, the branch of science that studies control systems in mechanical and electronic devices and compares them with biological systems to see which works better. A somewhat specialist branch of science, you might think, but that's what it does. The word was coined in the 1940s, but from the 1960s cyber- was adopted as a prefix by science-fiction writers (a cybernaut was a particularly nasty sort of robot and cyberculture a dehumanized vision of a future society). Then the Internet came along and made the cyber- world its own. Cyberspace was coined to mean "the notional place in which Internet communication takes place." This became so widespread that you can now shop at cybershops, have cybersex with a person you know only online, and buy a cyberpet, which is less likely than a guinea pig to upset the kids by dying.

Forum

"Forum" is Latin for "market place," and the forum was the focal point of Roman towns throughout the Empire. The law courts were in the forum, and it was here that public speeches were made, decisions were come to, and gossip of a political, commercial, or personal nature was exchanged. A forum, therefore, came to mean any arena (another word borrowed directly from the ancient Romans) where discussions were held, particularly legal ones: this is where the word "forensic" comes from. The term gradually broadened to embrace less formal discussions which, in recent decades, could take place online, without the need for the participants to be in the same room or, as we now call it, sharing **FACE TIME**.

Gatekeeper

"An individual who controls the flow of information into, within, or between organizations and decides who will be granted and who denied access." People who watched the gates of cities or castles in olden times had similar powers. For the last century or more, the metaphorical use has extended to those who control admission to colleges and universities, access to medical specialists, and the dissemination (or not) of information to the mass media. These days gatekeepers tend not to pour boiling oil on those who seek access to whatever they control, but otherwise they can be just as strict as their medieval equivalents.

Hardwired

If something is hardwired into a computer, it is fixed, unchangeable, and cannot be modified by any software that may later be added. Shortly after the expression was invented in the 1960s, it came to be used also for the bodily functions that are immovably associated with certain parts of the brain. Memory is linked to the cerebral cortex, breathing is controlled by the medulla oblongata, and there is nothing you can do about it. Thus hardwiring comes to be associated with inflexibility: "She was hardwired to go home at 5:30 sharp, whether the job was finished or not." You may feel this is meant to be discouraging, but the point about hardwiring is that all the discouragement in the world won't make a bit of difference. It is there, and it is there to stay.

In the Loop

In computing, a loop is a series of instructions within a program that the computer will perform over and over again until some specified condition is met; only then can it move on to its next function. In that context, "in the loop" was first found in the 1940s. By the 1970s it had broadened to include almost any sort of information: someone unable to attend an important meeting might be briefed afterward to keep her "in the loop." Conversely, if you don't want someone to be privy to confidential information, you can make a point of keeping her "out of the loop." (See also **(UP TO) SPEED**.)

Information Design

One of the more helpful concepts to emerge from the gobble-dygook that surrounds IT, information design means design that is focused on conveying information. On the understanding that a picture may be worth a thousand words, it frequently uses diagrams to illustrate unfamiliar concepts—and the better designed the diagram, the more easily the ill-informed will grasp the information. Thank you, whoever invented this. It's a good thing.

Information Overload

Put too much information into a computer and it will crash. Throw too much information at a person, and he or she will

collapse under the strain. Information overload is a concept that has been around for half a century but has become more serious since the advent of the Internet. Faced with the prospect of sifting through 20,461,356 hits on Google to find the kernel of information we need, most of us would be tempted to crash. When taken to extremes, this situation can lead to information fatigue syndrome, which has, since the 1990s, been recognized (surely satirically) as a disease that boils down to "Enough already!"

Input

In the sense of "a financial contribution, something put in," this dates back to the eighteenth century. For our purposes, however, it was co-opted into the world of computing in the 1940s to mean "the process of feeding in data, or the data itself." From there it spread out again to mean a contribution in the sense of an opinion: "We can't go ahead without asking the **STAKEHOLDERS** for their input." It's a perfectly pleasant, neutral word. There is no suggestion that the stakeholders are shoving their noses in where they aren't wanted (though goodness knows they do that often enough).

Knowledge Base

Although this has a specialist application in computing—"a collection of knowledge formulated for use in certain systems"—its broader meaning goes back further than that. As early as the 1950s, "knowledge base" was being used in business to mean any store of information on which decisions could be based. In those days it had a formal ring to it—the knowledge tended to be accumulated and made available in a structured manner. Nowadays it is more haphazard. An individual starting a new job may talk about "enhancing my knowledge base" to mean little more than "learning the details that are specific to this job as opposed to the very similar job I used to do." In other words, in everyday language it means more than just knowledge, but not much more. (See also **SKILL SET**.)

Malware

This is the technical term for computer viruses and the like—programs intended to be damaging or disruptive. It feels as if it should be an ultra-modern concept, belonging to the generation of Wikileaks, but in fact the *Merriam-Webster's* earliest example is dated 1990 and the concept had clearly been familiar to techies before then.

Orphan

Assuming you've seen *Oliver!*, even if you haven't read *Oliver Twist*, you probably think you know what an orphan is. But it is much more than a child who has lost its parents. The word has always been applied to a wide variety of things that have been deserted or neglected. In the 1970s "orphan" came to be used for diseases that affected so few people (or such poor people) that it was not economically viable for a drug company to re-search a cure. It now also refers to obsolete computer hardware and other non-biodegradable goods whose manufacturers have gone out of business and cannot take responsibility for dis-posing of them, to content whose copyright owners cannot be traced, and perhaps most worryingly, to the victims of firms ap-parently guilty of fraud that have since managed to disappear. Like *Oliver Twist*, these are all things that might be considered abandoned by someone who ought to be looking after them.

Paywall

Sometimes written as two words, this is the point on a web-site beyond which access to content ceases to be free. Many online newspapers and academic journals allow the casual browser to read an introductory paragraph or abstract, then charge for access to the entire article. The term, comprising two self-explanatory elements, is a recent one, coined in the early years of this century when the need for it arose.

Procurement

There was a time when "procuring" was inextricably linked with prostitution and a procuress was what Shakespeare's called a bawd. Then the word acquired a military sense—the procurement division in a First or Second World War army was in charge of acquiring equipment and supplies. Come the 1980s—that decade again—you could procure in the IT world

and now procurement has a broad remit, meaning "the acquiring of the appropriate goods and services at the best possible price so that everything is in the right place at the right time."

Straw Man Proposal

A modern version of **RUNNING IT UP THE FLAGPOLE TO SEE WHO SALUTES IT,** this is a proposal put forward to generate discussion and, one hopes, produce a better proposal. It's deliberately imperfect and—as the name suggests—easy to dispose of. The term originated not in anything to do with scarecrows, but in the development of the computer language

Ada in the 1970s. The early "strawman" draft was followed, as ideas became better thought-out and less liable to change, by woodenman, ironman, tinman, and others.

Technology Migration

The point about a migration, as opposed to a mere upgrade, is that old stuff to which you don't need to refer regularly is stashed away somewhere, so that you can access current material more quickly. One IT website tells us that "every technology migration project has a starting point in an existing system, and an end game in a new system, and the project is defined by the road that must be traveled to get from the existing system to the new one." In other words, it is somebody's job to know in advance (but presumably grossly underestimate) the amount of disruption the project will cause.

User-Friendly

A self-explanatory—or indeed user-friendly—expression, this means easy to use, designed so that you don't have to be an expert to work out what to do. From its first appearance in the 1970s it took less than a decade to spread beyond the computing world. You can now find "user-friendly" being applied to anything from life-insurance quotes (written in plain English) to recipes (using just a few ingredients and not expecting you to make a chocolate ganache before you start).

Viral Marketing

An odd term. You'd think viral marketing would be a bad thing, but no. It can generate massive sales. Since the arrival of social networks, you can tweet information about your product to all your friends, who pass it on to all their friends, who in turn . . . Thus, in the twinkling of an eye, everyone knows about your new widget and (in an ideal world) everyone is buying it. It has "gone viral."

Wiki

This is a Hawaiian word meaning quick. Hawaiian is one of those languages where you repeat a word for emphasis, so the name of the original wiki software, WikiWikiWeb, developed by Ward Cunningham of Oregon in the mid-1990s, meant that it was super quick. A wiki—of which the most famous is Wikipedia—is defined (by who else but Wikipedia itself?) as "a website that allows the creation and editing of any number of interlinked web pages via a web browser using a simplified markup language or a **WYSIWYG** text editor."

Ward never patented his idea. He is quoted as saying that he contemplated it but then thought, "If I got a patent I'd have to go out and sell people on the idea that anyone could edit. That just sounded like something that no one would want to pay money for." How wrong can you be?

9

Customer Value Orientation

MARKETING SPEAK

And finally . . . all this management is just fine, but you still have to sell the stuff. For that, there is another whole range of vocabulary that may leave the uninitiated baffled.

Big-Ticket Item

It is, of course, not the ticket that is big; it is the price written on it. A big-ticket item is by definition an expensive and non-essential purchase, the sort of product that will be bought only at times of **CONSUMER CONFIDENCE**. In that sense it has been around since 1945, but from the time of the American Civil War a big ticket had meant an honorable discharge from the armed services. For several hundred years on either side of the Atlantic, men discharged from the services or released from prison were given a ticket or warrant to show that they had done their time. A "small ticket" was a sign that a man had been dishonorably discharged. So a big-ticket item may be expensive and non-essential, but at least it is honorable.

In the early days of the metaphorical use, a big-ticket item was usually something like a refrigerator. Nowadays we also have "big-ticket lenders" (banks that will lend $20 million or more as a property investment). In the context of the US federal budget, such items as Medicare and Social Security, potential victims of cutbacks, have also been described as big-ticket. How honorable cutting them may be is another matter.

Brand Management

The earliest meaning of the word "brand" has to do with burning. As far back as the sixteenth century, a brand was a mark made on a farm animal with a burning iron to indicate whom it belonged to. From this it became an identifying mark on goods being shipped or marketed, from casks of brandy

to consignments of timber. By the mid-nineteenth century, it became a particular sort of goods, so that you could have a superior brand of anything from ale to candle wax. In the twentieth century, there evolved the concept of the brand name. With this, brand managers were hired to make sure the public was aware of the product—chocolate, soap powder, car, or whatever— and make the customer think one brand was superior to another by promoting it and its individual qualities.

The change that has come about in recent years has enabled a person to be a brand: Lady Gaga, Justin Bieber, anyone else of whom the public has a clear image and who is expected to **DELIVER** at a certain level. Whether the delivery is outlandish clothes and less outlandish songs or cheerful recipes for entertaining friends, the public knows what to expect.

As any brand manager will tell you, however, brands do occasionally need to be "refreshed," "repositioned," or "rebranded." But you need to get it right. Just as launching a new version of a soft drink when the public liked the old one can be an expensive disaster, so the career of a human brand can crash after, say, an ill-judged appearance on a reality TV show.

Bundling

A bundle, of course, is a number of things loosely wrapped together, like the belongings of a cartoon bum wrapped in a handkerchief on a pole over the shoulder. But bundling was borrowed by the computing world to mean selling hardware and software together in the same **PACKAGE** (not, by this time, necessarily in a handkerchief), and from there its use extended into other areas of sales and marketing where more than one product or service were supplied together. So a company selling cars could also provide a "bundle" that included insurance and a "free" 5,000 mile service, while a painter and decorator's "bundle" could include the delivery of carpets and curtains. According to the advocates of bundling, the practice benefits all concerned. The customer has the convenience of "one-stop shopping" and only one person to complain to if things go wrong, while the seller has the satisfaction of knowing that he has increased his **CUSTOMER VALUE ORIENTATION**.

Commoditization

According to one marketing expert, "An unrelenting change in technology, in addition to well-informed customers and fast-moving competition, has made sure that many once unique products or services have rapidly lost their intrinsic differentiation value and become 'commoditized.'" Companies that once enjoyed strong **BRANDING** now find their competitors producing similar or better offerings and suffer from "the resulting pressure on prices and margins."

In other words, too many people are making the same sort of stuff, so unless you get your marketing right you are unlikely to make money. The trick is to pursue value-added strategies (see **VAR**), stretch beyond core products, and offer customers compellingly differentiated values. But of course you knew that.

Consumer Backlash

Consumer backlash happens when the public takes a disliking to a product, perhaps because it is perceived to be "too popular." Heavily oaked Australian chardonnay, for example—the thing to drink in the 1980s—fell from favor in the 1990s, probably for no better reason than that it was "very '80s." Alternatively, consumers may start hating on a form of marketing. Being bombarded with random advertisements every time you log on to your e-mail may be so annoying that it turns you against the product being advertised as a matter of principle, rather than because you have any views on the product itself.

A backlash was originally a jarring movement caused by ill-fitting parts of machinery; by the early twentieth century it had attained its current, figurative meaning of a violent reaction against, well, anything really, from a political movement to a song that's beloved one day and played out the next.

Consumer Confidence

This has been around in the marketing world since the early twentieth century. It is applied either to a specific product that customers will buy because they trust it or to the more general condition of people being prepared to go out and spend money on non-essential, **BIG-TICKET ITEMS**—the "boom" element of a "boom or bust" economy.

Consumer Durable

See **FMCG**.

Consumer Headwind

This metaphorical meaning of headwind used in this phrase hasn't made it into any of my dictionaries—perhaps stores just made it up in 2008—but it is easy to see what it means. The poor customer is bravely battling against such difficulties as the credit crunch, increased VAT, and the temptation to stay home and shop online (see **FOOTFALL**). So just as a cyclist struggles against a strong wind or a football team finds the forces of nature are against it after changing sides at halftime, so do retailers find themselves trudging forward through customer resistance.

Courtesy Call

Invariably preceded by the words, "This is just a . . ." this ranks high on any list of "things I don't want to hear" in the modern world. It means that you already subscribe to a service or own a product produced by the caller's company and they want you to buy another, more expensive one (they may call it "upgrading," but don't be fooled). It's the telephonic equivalent of going into the post office to buy a stamp and being offered home insurance and a new credit card at the same time. Grrr.

Critical Mass

This is a term from nuclear physics and means "the minimum mass of fissile material that can sustain a nuclear chain reaction." It's used in business—mainly by people who wouldn't recognize fissile material if it was handed to them on a large hadron collider—to mean what is needed (in terms of sales or market share) to achieve profitability. Critical mass may also appear in a variety of other contexts. The critical mass of public opinion, for example, might cause the government to rethink a policy. In sociology it means the point at which a change has sufficient momentum to become unstoppable. In physics the expression dates from the 1940s; its wider use is much more recent.

Critical Mass is also the name of several bands, several albums, a couple of video games, and a worldwide bicycling event, none of which is relevant here.

Crowdsourcing

An article by Jeff Howe in a 2006 issue of *Wired* magazine described "the new pool of cheap labor" as "everyday people using their spare cycles to create content, solve problems, even do corporate R & D." It went on to say that "technological advances in everything from product design software to digital video cameras are breaking down the cost barriers that once separated amateurs from professionals . . . smart companies in industries as disparate as pharmaceuticals and television [are discovering] ways to tap the latent talent of the crowd."

This phenomenon is called crowdsourcing (almost invariably without the hyphen that it cries out for) and has rapidly expanded from practical work to various forms of decision-making. In 2011, the public was asked to vote for the next flavor of Ruffles potato chips. Far from muttering into their a bag of cheese and onion chips that this was what R & D departments were paid for, a million people—incentivized by a twenty-year supply of free chips—realized that they had nothing better to do with their time than vote for snack food. It is as frightening a sign of the times as any expression in this book.

As a matter of interest, I draw your attention to the expression "spare cycles" at the start of this entry. This has been defined as "the untapped human potential that explains why Wikipedia has over three and a half million entries in English:" blogging and loading the story of their lives on to Facebook and YouTube have given many people a creative outlet they have never had before. And why "cycles"? Well, it's a term from computing and refers to the parts of the computer that can be used to perform function B if it is not working to capacity performing function A. Untapped potential, in other words, which is where we came in.

Customer Value Orientation

Marketing speak for "doing what the customer wants." How well does your organization respond to customer needs? How long does the customer have to wait before receiving the goods or services you provide? Are they generally happy with those goods and services once they receive them? Basically, how good are you at keeping the customer satisfied? Pretty obvious stuff with a fancy name. Notice the absence of a hyphen, which makes the literal meaning harder to analyze. Is it "orientation to give the customer more value" or "orientation of value specifically for the customer"? Come to think of it, neither of those makes much sense, so perhaps it is better without the hyphen after all.

If, by the way, customer value orientation is so important to you that you work on the basis that the customer is always right, you may not go wrong but you will be guilty of misquotation. What César Ritz, founder of the Ritz hotels, actually said was, "The customer is never wrong." (Well, yes, OK, what he *really* actually said was, "*Le client n'a jamais tort*," but that is nit-picking.) It's a petty distinction, perhaps, but it forms part of a list of "famous things that were never said," along with "Play it again, Sam" and "Come up and see me sometime."

What Monsieur Ritz thought about *l'orientation du valeur livrée au client* is not recorded. My guess, though, is that he would have thought it was as meaningless in French as it is in English.

Downstream

See **UPSTREAM**.

Elevator Pitch

Imagine yourself arriving at work one morning, bursting with a bright, new idea. You reach the elevator at just the

same moment as the head of department who would have to **BUY INTO** this idea if it were ever to be taken seriously. You almost never have the chance to speak to this person directly—there are several tiers of management between you. Going through the usual formalities would take months and you would miss the all-important Christmas market. His office is on the twelfth floor. That gives you precisely eighteen seconds to grab his attention and put your idea across.

If you now find yourself goggling at his receding back, you didn't have an elevator pitch.

The word "pitch" in the sense of "spiel, sales talk" dates back to 1876 and probably originates in the fairground where the showman's patter was designed to make you part with your nickels and dimes in order to see the bearded lady. The more structured package of proposals that, say, an advertising agency uses in the hopes of winning a contract emerged in the 1960s, and honing your pitch to the length of a mere elevator ride length was popularized in the 1980s. The elevator pitch is now regarded as such a key feature of business and personal presentation that you can learn the art of it through the Harvard Business School and other distinguished institutions.

End User

When marketing speak created the **SUPPLY CHAIN**, it also created several tiers of customers. The company that produces components sells them to the company that produces the finished goods (and there may be more than one link in this part of the chain); the manufacturer then sells to a wholesaler who sells to a retailer. All these people are customers of the individual sellers. So when the retailer finally sells to his customer—the person who will take the dishwasher home and put dirty dishes in it—that person is distinguished by the title of "end user," an expression that has been around since the 1960s. If the end user eats or otherwise consumes the product (in which case it is unlikely to be a dishwasher), he is also a consumer and as such capable of generating **CONSUMER BACKLASH** or **CONSUMER CONFIDENCE**.

Focus Group

Widely used in all areas of market research, a focus group is a select group of people brought together to focus on a given subject or product. The group may be asked what they think of an existing product or, at an earlier stage of development, what they would like the product to **DELIVER**. Unfortunately focus groups resemble **STAKEHOLDERS** in that their interests are not necessarily aligned: the wishes and opinions of the marketing department, say, may seem completely pie in the sky to the production department whose job it is to deliver the goods.

The idea of a focus group evolved from the work of American sociologist Robert K. Merton (1910–2003) at Columbia University's Bureau of Applied Social Research. According to the *New York Times* obituary:

His adoption of the focused interview to elicit the responses of groups to texts, radio programs, and films led to the "focus groups" that politicians, their handlers, marketers, and hucksters now find indispensable. Long after he had helped devise the **METHODOLOGY**, Mr. Merton deplored its abuse and misuse but added, "I wish I'd get a royalty on it."

Professor Merton obviously had an eye for a catchy phrase: he is also credited with the invention of the role model and the self-fulfilling prophecy.

Footfall

"People going into stores," as in "retailers suffered a dramatic drop in footfall because of the bad weather before Christmas." In this sense footfall is a coinage from the late 1990s or early 2000s. As far as "the high street" is concerned it is made particularly relevant not only by people failing to go out in the snow but more permanently by the rise in online shopping. Black Friday in 2011 saw sales of $11.4 billion in stores and $1.4 billion spent online on Cyber Monday. Even though people spent almost ten times on Friday than Monday, the shoppingest days of the year, that's still a billion dollars worth of feet that aren't falling anywhere near a shopping mall.

High-End

This is recorded as meaning "sophisticated, likely to appeal to the wealthy or more discerning buyer" as early as the 1970s.

Its opposite is "low end," while "bottom end" is the same as "big end," the larger end of a connecting rod in an engine, and need not concern us here. In the UK, they used equivalents of these terms, "upmarket" and "downmarket," which were coined at about the same period and for a long time we had different words on different sides of the pond. Not any more: I recently saw "high-end" applied to that most British of commodities, marmalade.

(Out of) Left Field

We are back to baseball. Imagine that you are the batter, standing at the plate and facing the pitcher—the outfielder to your left is left field. Because he is in the outfield, he does not

play a pivotal role in every phase of the game and may even occasionally **(TAKE HIS) EYE OFF THE BALL**.

The concept of a person being figuratively "left field" and therefore disconnected with reality dates back to the middle of the twentieth century. From this developed "a left-field suggestion," meaning a bizarre one; and nowadays a suggestion may also "come out of left field," meaning that it appears out of nowhere and isn't a logical development of anything that has gone before.

But why should left field be more off the wall, as it were, than right field? Right-handed batters hitting the ball cleanly are likely to send it into left or center field, so you might think that the right outfielder would be the one who was most adrift from reality. Wikipedia's "Glossary of English language idioms derived from baseball" (yes, really, there is such a thing) offers several possible explanations, including a complicated one about the legendary Babe Ruth being left-handed and fans buying tickets for the wrong side of the stadium, but frankly these accounts aren't very satisfactory. Perhaps the expression just latches on to the deeply ingrained view that left (i.e., sinister, gauche) is by definition weirder than right.

Managing Expectations

All surprises should be good surprises, they say in the PR world, and the best way to achieve this is to under-promise and over-deliver. In other words, work out what you are absolutely confident of being able to achieve, promise a bit less, and then do better. Your customers will be thrilled, because you have managed their expectations. But of course they don't know that.

The prime example of managing expectations—attributed to the powers that be at Disneyland—is to put a sign saying, "Waiting time from here 45 minutes" at the point from which the waiting time is 30 minutes. Customers reach the front of the line much sooner than they expected, they are delighted, lavish compliments proliferate, God's in his heaven, and all's right with the small, small world.

Mass Sampling

If you've ever bought a magazine with a tiny packet of moisturizer attached to it, or had a bottle of an unfamiliar brand of mineral water thrust at you at a train station, you know what mass sampling is, even if you didn't know it had a name. It means handing out samples to the masses, or possibly handing out masses of samples, or both. It's a comparatively recent marketing ploy, common in the FMCG world, to encourage potential customers to try a commodity and, in an ideal world, fall in love with it and buy it avidly for ever more.

Missionary Selling

Sounds vaguely risqué, doesn't it? Or might it be something done on a wing and a prayer? In fact, this is a marketing term that has been recognized for twenty years or more, defined as "selling in which the salesperson's role is to build up goodwill rather than to make a direct sale." The concept is often applied to a product the customer has never tried before—life insurance, perhaps, or a pension scheme—and is about creating confidence, although obviously with the ultimate end of increasing sales. Why missionary? Well, it's because a missionary seller is going out into uncharted territory, marketwise, with a view to making the heathen masses (potential new customers) have faith in a new concept. And hoping you don't end up in the cooking pot.

Narrowcasting

First there was broadcasting, coined in the 1920s when radio was in its infancy, to mean scattering your message widely to reach the maximum possible audience. Then, shortly afterward, along came narrowcasting, a system whereby radio signals were not sent out around the full 360 degrees, but restricted to a narrower angle so that programs were not transmitted to sparsely populated areas. It seems odd in these high-tech days, but presumably it saved money. In this sense the word has more or less died out, only to be revived in the days of cable TV to mean targeting your audience—selling shopping channels to people who are interested in shopping, say, or, as the jargonistas put it, "niche marketing rather than mass marketing."

Offer

In the sense of "an act of offering, something on offer," this goes back five centuries before Mario Puzo's "offer he can't refuse." In newspeak, however, it has become an abbreviation for "things offered for sale," particularly in the sense of a range of goods that defines a company's image or ethos (see **CORPORATE DNA**). In bookselling terms, for example, what a supermarket has on "offer" is very different from that of a specialist bookshop. Or a French-style patisserie's "offer" differentiates it from a café specializing in bacon sandwiches and mugs of tea. If you are buying property or contemplating marriage, the word has its own particular—and potentially binding—implications, so be careful how you use it.

Penetration

Whatever other implications this word may have, in marketing speak it is entirely desirable but completely unconnected with sex (see **MISSIONARY SELLING** for another example of an expression that isn't smutty after all). It has been used since the 1960s to describe the extent to which a product or innovation has been sold into a particular market. Susan Wojcicki of Google, talking about new marketing opportunities for her organization, was quoted in 2010 as saying, "These smartphones have not been around for that long . . . Penetration is still growing," meaning, presumably, that not everyone has bought one yet, but they soon will.

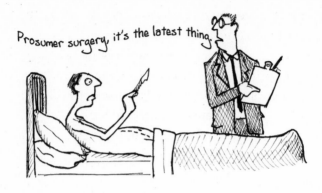

Prosumer

Prosumers—an amalgam of producers and consumers—
were coined by "futurist" Alvin Toffler in his 1980 book *The
Third Wave.* By "third wave" he meant the post-industrial society that was in its infancy at the time, following the first
and second waves of agricultural and industrial society. In
an agricultural society, Toffler maintained, everyone was a
prosumer—they grew their own food, built their own home,
etc. Once they began to produce a surplus (the beginnings of
industrialization), more and more people became consumers,
buying things that other people had produced. The development of the marketplace produced a very different society in
which everyone was dependent on everyone else: "The failure
of a major steel mill or glass factory to deliver needed supplies to an auto plant could, under certain circumstances,
send repercussions throughout a whole industry or regional
economy."

Are you with me so far? OK, now we hit the decline of

industrialization and the birth of the technological age. And all sorts of interesting things happen. People have more leisure, so they take up DIY. Putting together an entertainment center from IKEA—doing part of the job for the producer—is a form of prosumerism. Technology advances. Toffler cites the home pregnancy test as an early example of people taking some of their health care into their own hands, since previously such a test had had to be done by a doctor or lab technician. Self-help groups grow up. People who want to give up smoking, change their bad eating habits, or who find being the parents of twins exhausting, go not to the doctor or a paid therapist, but to a support group organized by fellow "sufferers." They are going back to a form of self-sufficiency, shifting from being "passive consumer to active prosumer."

Toffler predicted many of the changes that have taken place over the last thirty years, but he didn't quite envisage the phenomenon of **WIKI**, which takes prosumerism a step further. As executive coach James Caplin puts it in his book *I Hate Presentations* (2008), "We used to have encyclopedias. They, the knowledgeable, shared their wisdom with us, the ignorant. It was an adult-to-child interaction. We now have Wikipedia. We, the knowledgeable ones, share our information with each other." In the twenty-first century we are back where our ancestors were over a thousand years ago; we are not only productive but **PROACTIVE** consumers.

Pull Marketing

The old-fashioned approach was sometimes called "push marketing"—you got out there into the marketplace, told people how wonderful your stuff was, and they bought it. Pull marketing is more subtle than that. It lures the customer in with "buy me now" offers that sound like a bargain ("two for the price of one") but also give a sense of urgency ("while stocks last," "must end Friday"). This idea has really come into its own since the invention of online networking. Potential clients can visit your website, read your blog, take note of your special offers, and decide that yours is the sort of company they want to do business with. Won't you come into my parlor, as the spider said to the fly.

Real Time

In the early days of computing, doing something "in real time" meant there and then, giving results more or less instantly rather than analyzing or processing them later. Latterly the term has been adopted by the marketing world, so that "real-time marketing" means "responding very quickly to the needs of the marketplace or customer." The blurb for David Meerman Scott's book *Real-time Marketing and PR: How to Instantly Engage Your Market, Connect with Customers, and Create Products That Grow Your Business Now* (2010) explains it with remarkably little drivel and a commendable absence of exclamation marks: "Gone are the days when you could plan out your marketing and public relations programs well in advance and release them on your timetable. It's a real-time world now, and if you're not engaged, then you're on your way to marketplace irrelevance. 'Real time' means news breaks over minutes, not days. It means ideas percolate, then suddenly and unpredictably go **VIRAL** to a global audience . . . it's when businesses see an opportunity and are the first to act on it."

So what are you sitting here for? Stop wasting real time, and get out there!

Running It Up the Flagpole

In the film *Twelve Angry Men*, set in a jury room, one of the jurors is a brash young advertising man who tells a story about **BRAINSTORMING** sessions at his agency. When a deadlock arises, one of his colleagues will always say, "Here's an idea. Let's run it up the flagpole and see if anyone salutes it." The character relating this thinks it is a marvelous example of **THINKING OUTSIDE THE BOX**: "I mean, it's idiotic," he says admiringly, "but it's funny, huh?"

That was in 1957 and clearly the image—meaning to float an idea to see if anyone thinks it is any good—was new to the other jurors he was talking to. Nowadays you don't have to use the full expression for people to know what you mean; a sure sign that it has descended into the realm of clichés.

Later in the film, the same indefatigably cheerful character comes up with another idea, which he prefaces with, "Let's throw it out on the stoop and see if the cat licks it up," an expression which seems, mercifully, not to have caught on.

And, maybe it was just Hollywood, maybe it was that line of work that required lots of variations on the same theme, but in the 1962 film *Days of Wine and Roses* a PR executive suggests that he "pull something out of the hat and see if it hops for us." Was it the innate hint of patriotism that made "run it up the flagpole" win out against such strong competition?

Spin

Baseball pitchers put a spin on the ball to control its direction and make it more difficult for the batter to "read." This may be where the modern sense—of putting a particular slant on a piece of news or government policy—originated: the person doing the spinning controls where the information goes and how it is interpreted. The expression emerged in American politics in the late 1970s, and political public relations officers were rebranded as "spin doctors" shortly afterward. Why "doctor" (as opposed to, say, "artist," by analogy with "con artist"), it is difficult to say, but it is worth noting that "to doctor" in the sense of "to alter the appearance of, to tamper with or 'cook'" has been in use since the eighteenth century and shows no signs of going away.

Supply Chain

The supply chain originated in military speak as the route by which an army received its supplies. In that sense it is over a hundred years old. Its use in the business context dates back to the 1950s, and ever since then it has meant the chain of processes involved in the production of a commodity and its journey toward its **END USER**. (See also **DELIVERY** and **UPSTREAM/DOWNSTREAM**.)

Upstream/Downstream

By the 1970s these words were no longer confined to rivers; they had spread out into the oil industry to describe the "flow" of the various stages of the process. The upstream elements are exploration and research and the downstream ones are refining, distribution, and marketing. Nowadays upstream or downstream activities can take place in any business, either within a corporation or between a number of companies which form part of the same **SUPPLY CHAIN**. Within a corporation, an upstream loan, for example, is a loan from a subsidiary company to its holding company, given because the latter doesn't have a good enough credit rating to borrow money elsewhere. In the supply-chain context, upstream refers to the manufacturers of components and suppliers of materials. Downstream from them are those who put the components together, and then finally the various levels of customers (see **END USERS**) are the most downstream of all.

Acknowledgments

When I started talking about writing this book, a number of friends said, "Oh, you must include . . ." normally followed by, "That really annoys me." So building up a contents list was, as it has been before, a communal effort. Particular thanks are due this time to Alex, Carol, and Lorraine for working in the sort of jobs where this vocabulary is rampant. Thanks also to Louise, Ana, and everyone else at Michael O'Mara for continuing to **FIRE ON ALL CYLINDERS**.

Bibliography

This book couldn't have been written without the brilliant people who compile the *Oxford English Dictionary* and the kind ones at Westminster Libraries who allow me to view it online. Many of the definitions are based on my beloved *Chambers Dictionary 2008*, the *Collins English Dictionary* and the online *Merriam-Webster Dictionary* (www.merriam-webster.com).

I have also drawn inspiration and information from the following books and sites.

Caplin, James. *I Hate Presentations.* Chichester, UK: Capstone, 2008.

Cresswell, Julia. *The Cat's Pyjamas: The Penguin Book of Clichés.* London: Penguin, 2007.

Ellis, Simon and Janet Tod. *Behaviour and Learning.* New York: Routledge, 2009.

Fugere, Brian, Chelsea Hardaway and Jon Warshawsky. *Why Business People Speak Like Idiots: A Bullfighter's Guide.* New York: Free Press, 2005.

Green, Jonathon. *Dictionary of Jargon.* Routledge and Kegan Paul, 1987.

Kashani, Kamran, ed. Beyond *Traditional Marketing: Innovations in Marketing Practice*. Hoboken: John Wiley & Sons, 2005.

Scott, David Meerman. *Real-Time Marketing and PR*. Hoboken: Wiley, 2010.

Sturgeon, Ron. *Green Weenies and Due Diligence*. Lynden, WA: Mike French Publishing, 2005.

Toddler, Alvin. *The Third Wave*. New York: William Morrow, 1980.

Thorne, Tony. *Shoot the Puppy*. Penguin reference. 2006.

Whichelow, Clive and Hugh Murray. *It's Not Rocket Science and Other Irritating Modern Clichés*. Portrait, 2007.

www.jrank.org/business

www.phrases.org.uk/meanings

http://searchenterprisewan.techtarget.com

Index

ENJOY THESE OTHER
READER'S DIGEST BESTSELLERS

I Used to Know That

Make learning fun again with these lighthearted pages that are packed with important theories, phrases, and those long-forgotten "rules" you once learned in school.

Caroline Taggart
ISBN 978-0-7621-0995-1

A Certain "Je Ne Sais Quoi"

A smorgasbord of foreign words and phrases used in everyday English—from Aficionado (Spanish) to Zeitgeist (German). Inside you'll find translations, definitions, and origins that will delight and amuse language lovers everywhere.

Cloe Rhodes
ISBN 978-1-60652-057-4

An Apple a Day

Discover the origins and meanings of proverbs—those colorful time-honored truths that enrich our language and culture. You'll learn why these sayings have stood the test of time.

Caroline Taggart
ISBN 978-1-60652-191-5

Spilling the Beans on the Cat's Pajamas

This book spills the beans on our best-loved euphemisms and most curious sayings and the remarkable stories that surround them. It rounds up the hundreds of catch phrases and expressions that enrich our everyday speech and makes them easy to find in an A-to-Z format.

Judy Parkinson
ISBN 978-1-60652-171-7

i before e (except after c)

Featuring all the memory-jogging tips you'll ever need to know, this fun book will help you recall hundreds of important facts using simple, easy-to-remember mnemonics from your schooldays.

Judy Parkinson
ISBN 978-0-7621-0917-3